GW01315789

IELTS ACADEMIC WRITING TASK 1 SAMPLES

50 High Quality Samples for Your Reference to Gain a High Band Score 8.0+ In 1 Week (Book 9)

RACHEL MITCHELL

Copyright © 2017

All rights reserved.

ISBN: 9781973163107

TEXT COPYRIGHT © [RACHEL MITCHELL]

all rights reserved. No part of this guide may be reproduced in any form without permission in writing from the publisher except in the case of brief quotations embodied in critical articles or reviews.

Legal & disclaimer

The information contained in this book and its contents is not designed to replace or take the place of any form of medical or professional advice; and is not meant to replace the need for independent medical, financial, legal or other professional advice or services, as may be required. The content and information in this book have been provided for educational and entertainment purposes only.

The content and information contained in this book have been compiled from sources deemed reliable, and it is accurate to the best of the author's knowledge, information, and belief. However, the author cannot guarantee its accuracy and validity and cannot be held liable for any errors and/or omissions. Further, changes are periodically made to this book as and when needed. Where appropriate and/or necessary, you must consult a professional (including but not limited to your doctor, attorney, financial advisor or such other professional advisor) before using any of the suggested remedies, techniques, or information in this book.

Upon using the contents and information contained in this book, you agree to hold harmless the author from and against any damages, costs, and expenses, including any legal fees potentially resulting from the application of any of the information provided by this book. This disclaimer applies to any loss, damages or injury caused by the use and application, whether directly or indirectly, of any advice or information presented, whether for breach of contract, tort, negligence, personal injury, criminal intent, or under any other cause of action.

You agree to accept all risks of using the information presented inside this book.

You agree that by continuing to read this book, where appropriate and/or necessary, you shall consult a professional (including but not limited to your doctor, attorney, or financial advisor or such other advisor as needed) before using any of the suggested remedies, techniques, or information in this book.

TABLE OF CONTENT

INTRODUCTION

Thank you and congratulate you for downloading the book *"Ielts Academic Writing Task 1 Samples: 50 High Quality Samples for Your Reference to Gain a High Band Score 8.0+ in 1 Week (Book 9)."*

This book is well designed and written by an experienced native teacher from the USA who has been teaching IELTS for over 10 years. She really is the expert in training IELTS for students at each level. In this book, she will provide you 50 high quality sample essays to help you easily achieve an 8.0+ in the IELTS Writing Task 1 (Academic), even if your English is not excellent. These samples will also walk you through step-by-step on how to develop your well-organized answers for the Task 1 Writing.

As the author of this book, I believe that this book will be an indispensable reference and trusted guide for you who may want to maximize your band score in IELTS academic task 1 writing. Once you read this book, I guarantee you that you will have learned an extraordinarily wide range of useful, and practical IELTS WRITNG TASK 1 sample essays that will help you become a successful IELTS taker as well as you will even become a successful English writer in work and in life within a short period of time only.

Take action today and start getting better scores tomorrow!

Thank you again for purchasing this book, and I hope you enjoy it.

SAMPLE 1

The pie charts below give information about world population in 1900 and 2000.

Summarise the information by selecting and reporting the main features, and make comparisons where relevant.

World population by region, 1900 and 2000

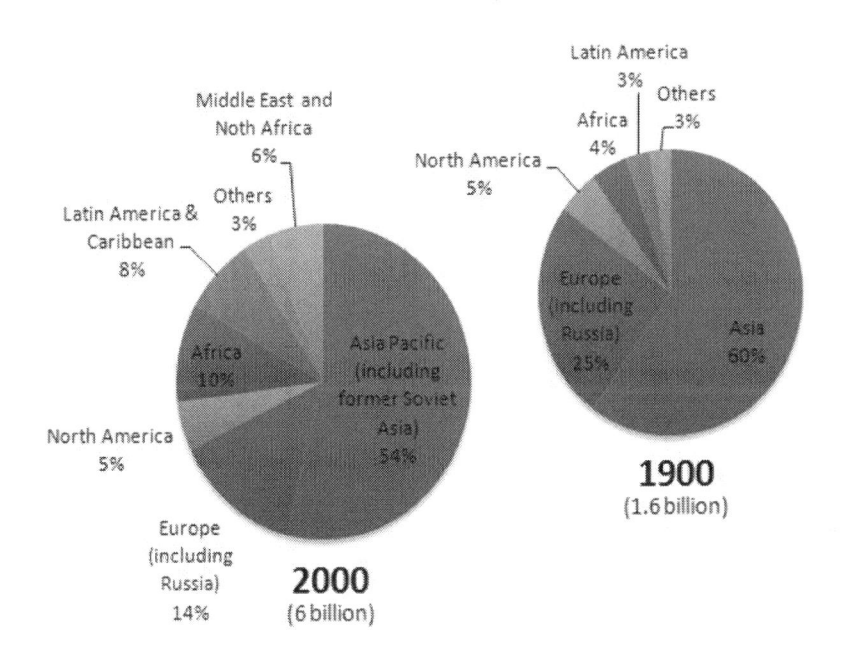

The pie charts illustrate changes in the percentages of the population of different areas of the world between 1900 and 2000.

Overall, there was a significant rise in the total number of the world population, from 1.6 billion to 6 billion over a century. Moreover, it is evident that the highest population rate belonged to nations in Asia in both years shown.

In 1990, Asia accounted for 60% of the world population which was the highest portion compared to the remaining. This was followed by Europe (including Russia) with a quarter (25%). Latin America and others each accounted for 3% of the total of world population rate.

Although this number dropped by 6% in 2000 to 54%, Asia still represented the largest population of the world. At the same time, the proportion of the population in Europe (including Russia) also showed the remarkable downward trend to just roughly 15%. By contrast, Africa and Latin experienced a significant growth in the number of inhabitants to 10% and 8% respectively. Meanwhile, over the period from 1900 to 2000, the percentage of the population in North America and other regions remained consistently unchanged at around 5% and 3%, while the figure for the Middle East and North Africa constituted a slightly higher portion of 6% which was just referred in 2000.

218 words

SAMPLE 2

The chart below shows global sales of the top five mobile phone brands between 2009 and 2013.

Write a report for a university, lecturer describing the information shown below.

Summarise the information by selecting and reporting the main features and make comparisons where relevant.

Global mobile phone sales by brand

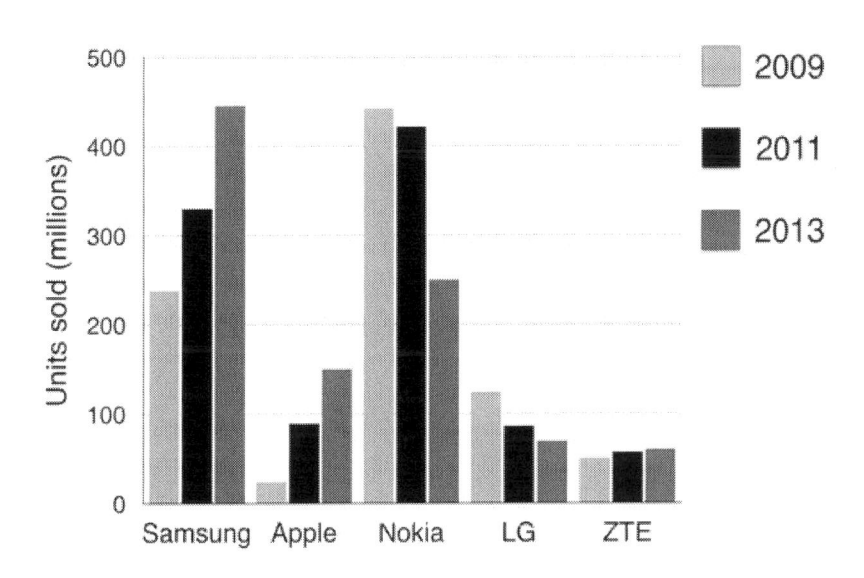

MODEL ANSWER 1:

The bar chart compares five cell phone companies in terms of their worldwide sales volume in the three consecutive odd years, 2009, 2011 and 2013.

Overall, Samsung and Nokia were the two dominant companies in the mobile phone industry. It is also evident that different trends in sales had been experienced by the five featured brands.

In 2009, Nokia had the highest international sales with approximately 430 million units sold, followed by Samsung, whose figure was only half that number, at around 230 million units. LG came third with about 120 million phones while sales of ZTE and Apple were at a negligible/paltry number. Two years later, both Samsung and Apple managed to boost their sales to 330 and 90 million units respectively. Incompatible with the established trend, Nokia and LG experienced a slight decrease in their sales volume.

2013 marked another dramatic rise of 100 million units in Samsung sales; meanwhile, Nokia suffered a fall of nearly 200 million phones and lost its dominant position to Samsung. Apple came third with its sales almost doubling the 2011 figure to 150 million phones. There had only been little changes in the sales volume of LG and ZTE.

197 words

MODEL ANSWER 2:

The bar chart illustrates the number of the cell phone from top five companies sold out around the world in 3 years 2009, 2011 and 2013.

Overall, all three band Samsung, Apple and ZTE increased their sale volumes while both Nokia and LG had a decline over the same period. In addition, Samsung and Nokia were the two biggest companies in the world by sale.

In 2009, the number of the cell phones sold out from Nokia was the highest at around 450 million units. By contrast, the figure for Apple was at the lowest point of about 20 million units. Approximately 240 million cell phones sold out by Samsung, compared to 120 million units of LG and 50 million of ZTE.

The sale volume of Samsung increased dramatically to around 450 million units in 2013, this brand now took over as Nokia as the biggest companies according to sale volume in the world. Similarly, Apple saw a significant growth in sales, the number for the year 2013 was 7.5 times more than that of 2009, from 20 million to 150 million phones. On the other hand, Nokia's global sale fell sharply by 200 million units, which was 250 million phones in 2013 and was just a half of the Samsung's sale volume. There was also a sharp decline in LG's global sale by 60 million units, falling to 70 million phones in 2013. The number of the phones sold out by ZTE generally remained stable at around 55 million over the period.

220 words

SAMPLE 3

You should spend about 20 minutes on this task.

The diagram below shows how geothermal energy is used to produce electricity.

Summarise the information by selecting and reporting the main features, and make comparisons where relevant.

Write at least 150 words.

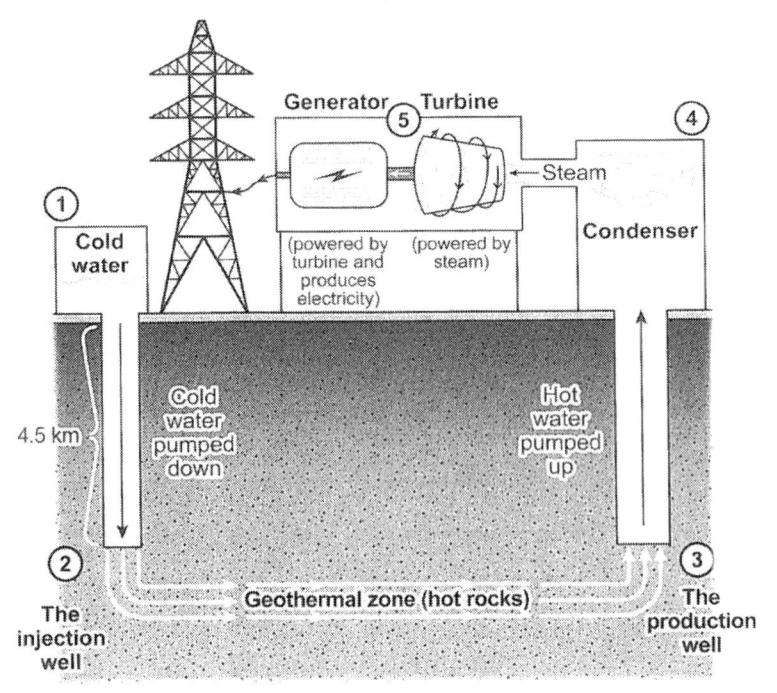

Geothermal power plant

The graph illustrates the process of generating electricity using geothermal energy in a power plant.

It is clear that there are five distinct stages in the process, beginning with pumping cold water down into the ground. In the final step, electricity produced is sent to the grid for the delivery.

At the first stage, cold water stored in a tank is pumped down into the injection well, which leads the liquid to the depth of 4.5 km below the ground. Cold water is then quickly warmed up by hot rocks while flowing through the geothermal zone. In the next step, hot water is brought back to the ground into the condense where the steam is stored.

The fourth stage of the process involves turning the turbine. The turbine, powered by the steam deriving from the condenser, rotates around an axis. As the generator is connected directly to the turning axis, it converts the movement power into electricity. At the last stage of the process, electricity is transferred to the grid to reach the users.

174 words

SAMPLE 4

The diagram below shows the average hours of unpaid work per week done by people in different categories. (Unpaid work refers to such activities as childcare in the home, housework, and gardening.)

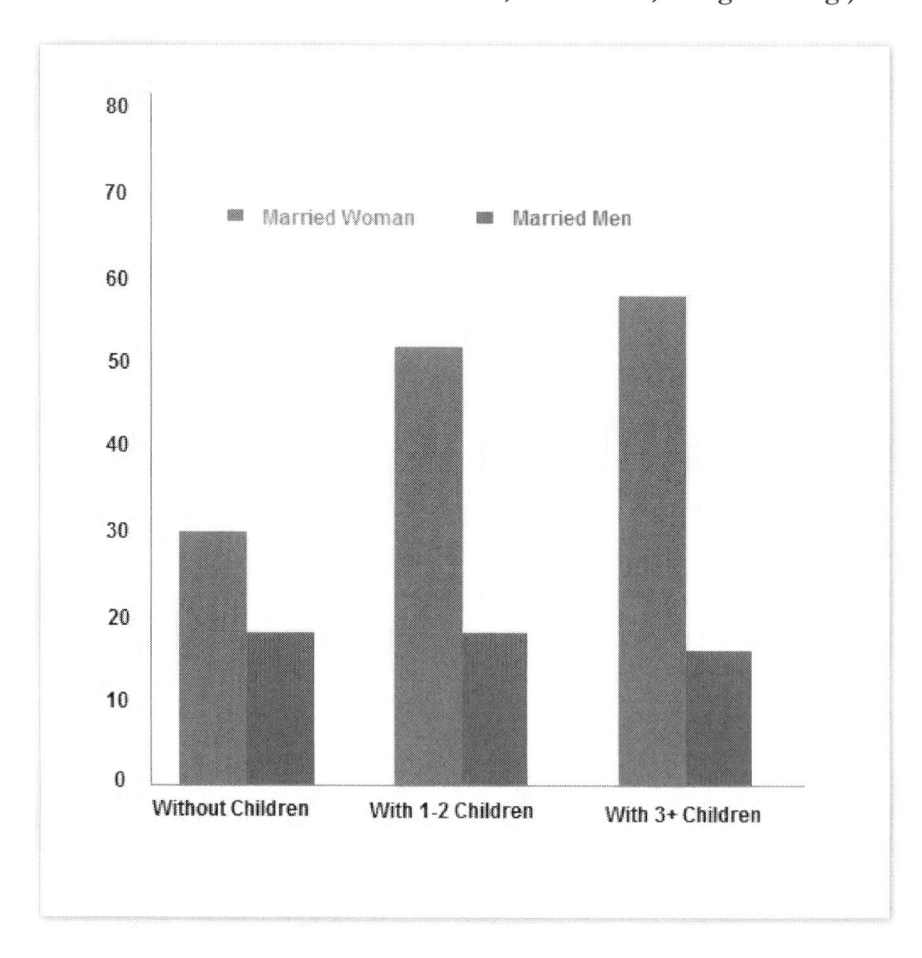

The bar chart illustrates data on the number of hours people spend on their unpaid work weekly, which is categorized by their gender and the number of children they have.

Overall, it is obvious that women spend more time doing housing activities rather than men. Moreover, the more children the households have, the more hours women spend on housework.

According to the chart, while non-child women spend approximately 30 hours per week, the figures for mothers with children are significantly higher. To be precise, about 50 and 60 hours spent on childcare, housework, and gardening are allocated to women who have 1-2 and above 3 children, respectively.

Meanwhile, men have a much smaller number of hours for home tasks, being halved of those of women in all three kinds of families. Besides, it is noticeable that the data shows a similar amount of 20 hours/week are spent on daily routine activities for males, regardless of the number of children they have.

161 words

SAMPLE 5

The chart and graph below give information about sales and share prices for Coca-Cola.

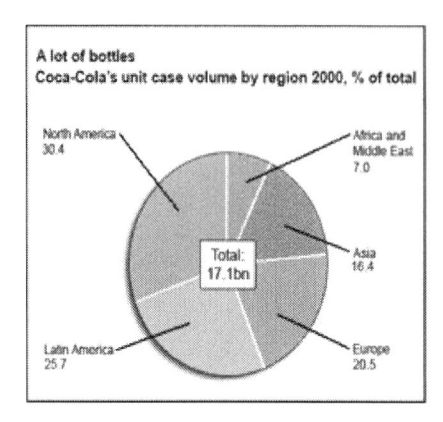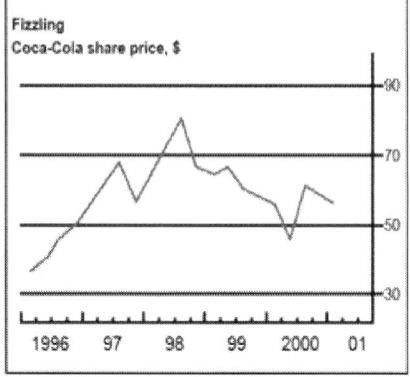

The pie chart presents data on how many bottles of Coca-cola were consumed by 5 different areas during 2000, while the line graph illustrates the share price changing over 6 years from 1996 to 2001.

In general, by far the highest expenditure of drinking Coca-cola came from North American country. The line graph shows the fluctuation of share-price of a soft drink.

It was clearly indicated from the pie chart that American nation consumed a large amount of beverage, which accounts for more than a half out of the total with 17.1 billion bottles and being divided into two areas from North America and Latin America which was 30.4 and a quarter respectively. In contrast, Africa and the Middle East saw a very small number of bottles, 7 percent. Of the remaining of this chart, the proportion of Coca-Cola's unit was sold in Europe and Asia respectively.

The line graph shows that the share price began at over 30 dollars then reached the highest peak at 80 dollars in the first 3 initial years. After that, there was followed by a period of stability decline before climbing again at the end in 2001.

194 words

SAMPLE 6

The graph below shows the amounts of waste produced by three companies over a period of 15 years.

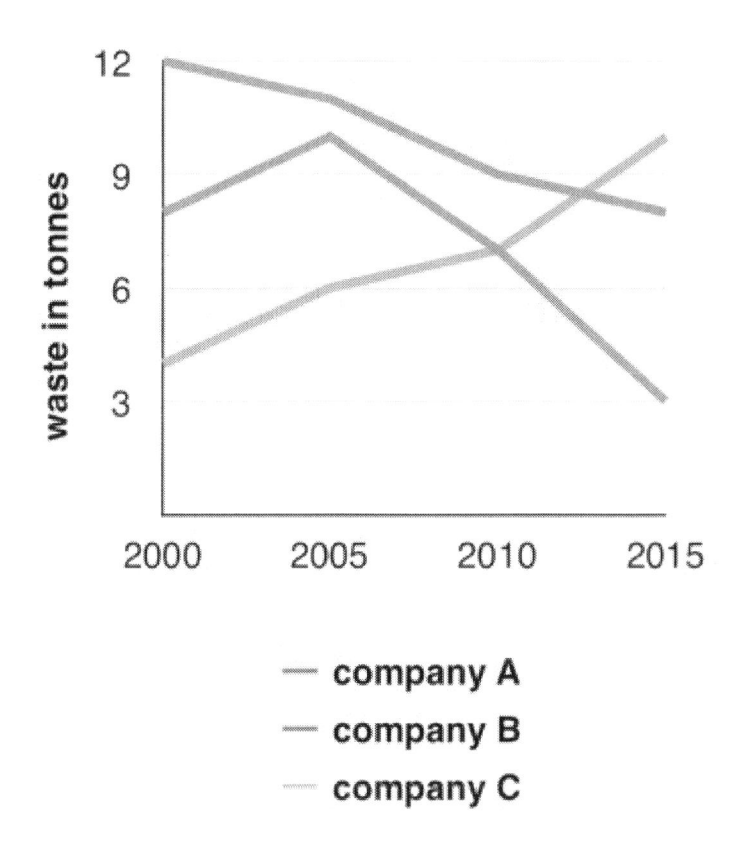

The graph illustrates data on how much waste was made by three organizations from 2000 to 2015.

Overall, company A and company B had the tendency to reduce their waste over the years while company C was likely to produce more waste during the given period.

Of the three companies, company A produced the largest amount of waste at accurately 12 tonnes in 2000. However, this figure fell constantly to reach its lowest point of approximately 8 tonnes in 2015. On the contrary, company C made about 4 tonnes of waste in 2000 followed by a swift increase by around 6 tonnes towards the end of the period.

Looking at the chart in more detail, 8 tonnes of waste was made by company B in 2000. After peaking at 10 tonnes in 2005, the amount of waste produced by company B plummeted to precisely 3 tonnes, making it the one with the smallest waste production in 2015.

157 words

SAMPLE 7

The following pie charts show the results of a survey into the most popular leisure activities in the United States of America in 1999 and 2009.

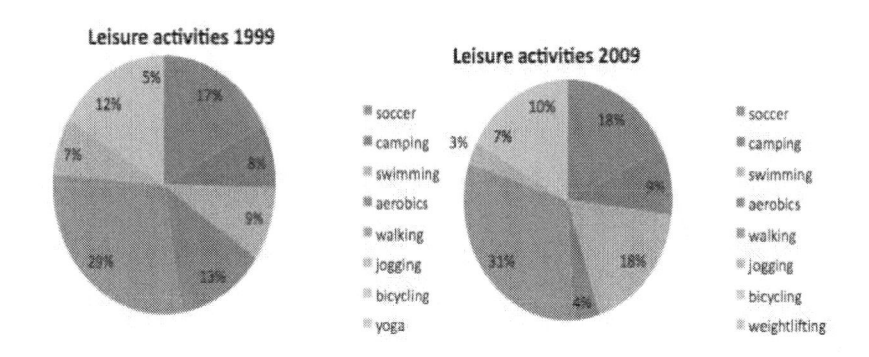

The pie charts compare the most American favorite recreations in two years 1999 and 2009.

It is obvious that walking and playing football accounted for the greatest percentage in both years.

In 1999, the percentage of walking, which was chosen as the favorite activity by the majority of American was 29%, while the rate for yoga was lowest, at only 5%. Besides, the figure for soccer was significantly lower, at 17%, followed by aerobics and bicycling at 13% and 12% respectively. Meanwhile, there was not much difference among the figure for jogging, camping and swimming from 7% to 9%.

In 2009, the rate of soccer was still highest, at 31%. After the period of 10 years, the proportion of American choosing swimming raised doubled to the same as football's figure, at 18%. Meanwhile, there was a rapid decrease seen in the percentage of people went jogging, rode bicycles and did aerobics. Especially, yoga was replaced by weightlifting and one in ten American people preferred weightlifting as a new leisure activity.

170 words

SAMPLE 8

The pie chart below shows information on the highest level of education of women in Someland in 1945 and 1995.

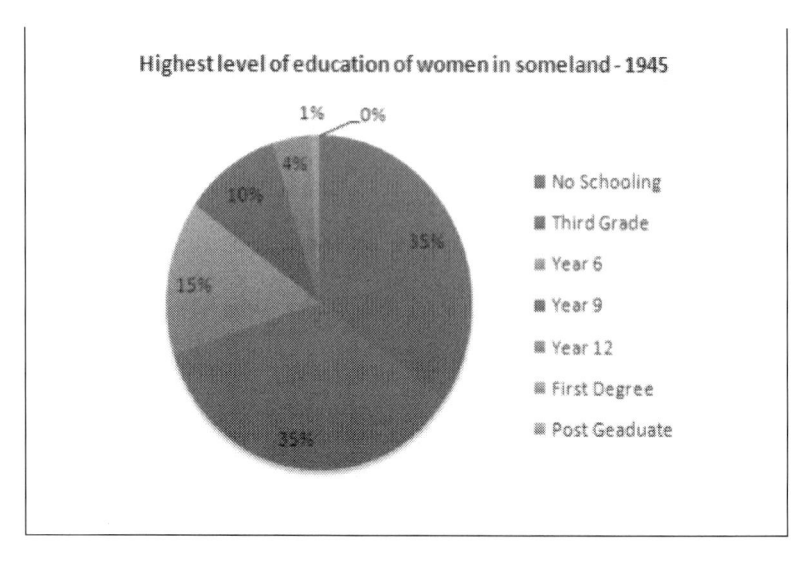

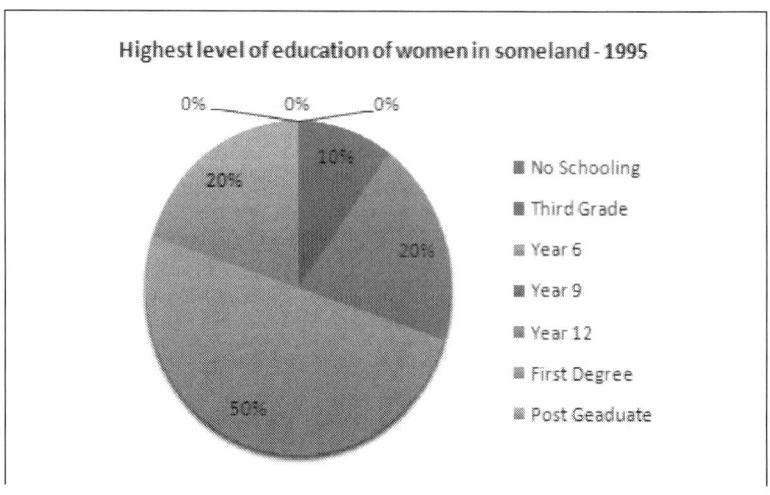

The given figure illustrates the changes regarding the highest educational level that females in Someland could reach in the year 1945 and 1995. The chart is measured in percentage.

Overall, while most women in Someland did not go to school or stopped their education before getting their first degree in 1945, half of the women in Someland managed to finish tertiary education while some even proceeded to a master degree.

In 1945, the number of women who did not attend school and dropped out of school after third grade each accounted for 35% of the total number of female citizens, making them the two most common education level of females at that time. In addition, the figure for female learners reaching sixth grade was only 15% and those who completed year 9, year 12 and obtained their first degree were just 10%, 4%, and 1%, respectively. Interestingly, none of them acquired post-graduate certificates.

However, in 1995, the trend completely changed with a sharp increase in the percentage of female school goers that were capable of achieving higher levels of education. Particularly, there were no female students who stopped their education at grade six and half of them successfully graduated from university. Also, compared with 1945, there was the same ratio of female ninth graders in 1995, at 10% and those who completed high school and post-graduate program each comprised one-fifth of the total number.

219 words

SAMPLE 9

The table shows the worldwide market share of the mobile phone market for manufacturers in the years 2005 and 2006.

Summarise the information by selecting and reporting the main features, and make comparisons where relevant.

Company	2005 % Market share	2006 % Market share
Nokia	32.5	35
Motorola	17.7	21.1
Samsung	12.7	11.8
Sony Ericsson	6.3	7.4
LG	6.7	6.3
BenQ Mobile	4.9	2.4
Others	19.2	16.2
TOTAL	100.0	100.0

A glance at the table provided illustrates data on the mobile phone producers in terms of their share of global market in the years 2005 and 2006

Overall, it is apparent that Nokia was the largest market share in both years. While the percentage of market share of Nokia, Motorola and Sony Ericson increased, that of the remainder companies fell.

As can be seen from the table, the most striking feature is that Motorola experienced the highest growth which rose by 3.4% from 17.7% in 2005 to reach 21.1% in 2006. Also, there was a slight increase in the percentage of market share of Nokia and Sony Ericsson which went up from 32.5 % and 6.3% in 2005 to 35% and 7.4% in 2006, respectively.

In a stark contrast, BenQ Mobile witnessed a sustainable decline which decreased from 4.9% in 2005 to 2.4% in 2006, a fall of 2.5% from the previous year. Similarly, Samsung and LG went down minimally from 12.7 % and 6.7% in 2005 to 11.8% and 6.3% in 2006 in that order. Finally, there was a dip in the market share of other companies by 3% to 16.2% in 2006.

194 words

SAMPLE 10

The diagram shows the changes that have taken place at West Park Secondary School since its construction in 1950.

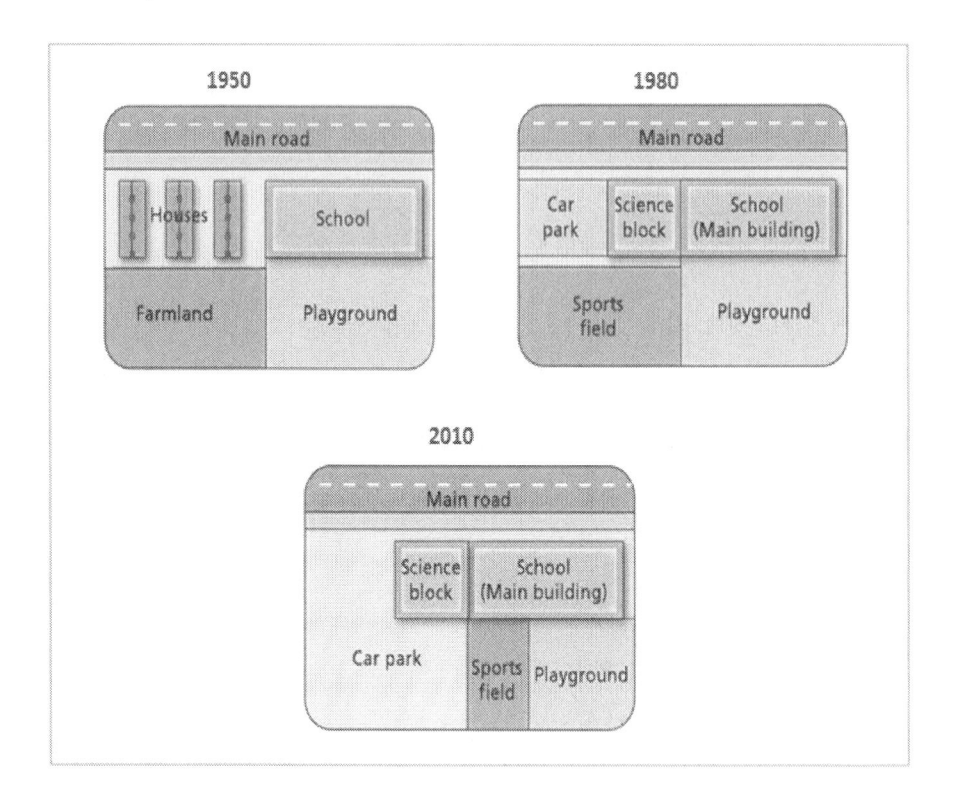

MODEL ANSWER 1:

The maps illustrate how a secondary school called West Park Secondary School changes considerably over a period of 60 years from 1950 to 2010.

Overall, though the main building itself remained the same, the school witnessed significant alterations in construction with the emergence of new facilities/amenities.

From 1950 to 1980, while the main building and the playground were still there, the houses were demolished to make way for an additional block of the school and a new car park whereas a sports field replaced the old farmland.

By 2010, the science block and the school had been stayed unchanged. The car park was widened a replaced the area of the sports field, leading to the sports field being diminished and moved into a small part of the playground area. As a result, the playground was reduced in size.

150 words

MODEL ANSWER 2:

The above diagrams provide information about West Park Secondary School's architectural transformations with three milestones: 1950, 1980 and 2010.

Overall, it can clearly be seen from these sources that the building complex had witnessed numerous changes in layouts since its original structure in 1950.

According to the first diagram, West Park Secondary School located next to three blocks of houses which had a farmland attached at the back in 1950. The school had a pretty large playground which neatly lied at the rear of its main building. However, in 1980, the school expanded itself on the left-hand side, converting the farmland into a new sports field and right in front of the sports field, a new car park and science block were built on the original land of the housing blocks.

The year 2010 showed that the school layout kept being modified into a somewhat more modern architecture, where the car park tripled its size & took a large portion of land from the sports field which had been relocated to become a small part of the playground as a result. The school's main building and science block, despite all these modifications, remained exactly the same in location & size compared to the 1980 structure.

205 words

SAMPLE 11

The two graphs show the main sources of energy in the USA in the 1980s and the 1990s.

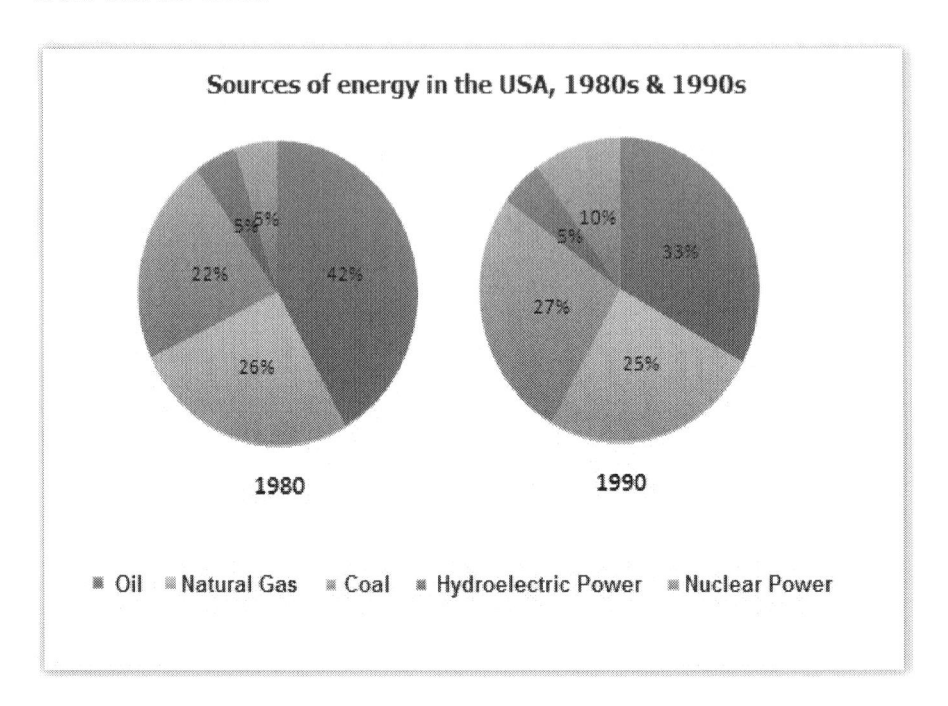

MODEL ANSWER 1:

The two pie charts illustrate data on percentages of several main energy sources, varying from the 1980s to 1990s in the USA.

Overall, there were predominant proportions allocated to oil during the 1980s as well as 1990s. Moreover, the rates of the remaining sources were obvious to remain relatively unchanged over the period.

During the 1980s, approximately 42% of total main energy sources were reported to be oil, whereas the minority of 5% of nuclear power was utilized for generating energy. However, a decade later, there was a reduction of 9% in the proportion of oil usage, at 33%. Meanwhile, the figure doubled to 10% for nuclear energy in the 1990s.

Apart from that, the rest 3 power sources were noticeable to maintain balanced or inconsiderably increase during those years, which was estimated about 25% for natural gas and 5% for hydrodynamic power. Moreover, a slight increase of 5% was reported in coal utilization, at 27% in the 1990s.

159 words

MODEL ANSWER 2:

The two pie charts compare the percentage of energy consumption from five different in the USA between 1980 and 1990.

Overall, oil and natural gas were the major sources of energy in the USA in both 1980 and 1990. Hydroelectric power in both years constituted the lowest figure for energy used in the USA.

It can be seen the most popular energy used in the USA was oil, at 42% in 1980. This was slightly higher than the oil consumption rate in 1990, at 33%. Following the coil usage, 26% of natural gas was consumed in 1980. After 10 years, the figure for natural gas almost remained unchanged, at 25%. There was a significant increase in the percentage of coal production from 22% in 1908 to 27%in 1990.

Hydroelectric power and nuclear power accounted for the lowest figures in the energy consumption rate with 5% in both years and an increase of 5%, respectively.

154 words

SAMPLE 12

The chart below shows how frequently people in the USA ate in fast food restaurants between 2003 and 2013.

Summarise the information by selecting and reporting the main features, and make comparisons where relevant.

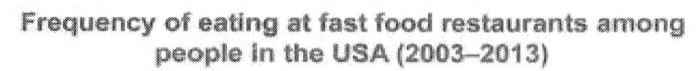

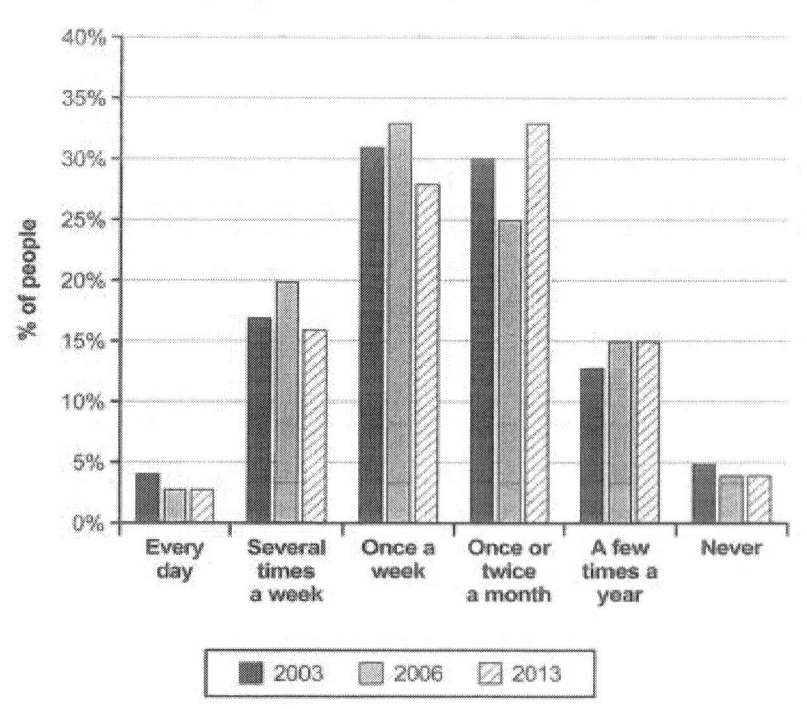

The bar chart illustrates the variation of eating at fast food restaurants among American residents/ citizens from 2003 to 2013.

It is clear that the rate of consumption of fast food rose steadily from frequency in every day to peak of roughly once a week and once or twice a month and then tailing off to never. On the other hand, it was a temporal variation into each group during the period of 2003 – 2013.

We can see that the general trend is for the number of people who have never or daily eaten at fast food restaurants to decrease and stable from 2003 to 2013 (under 5 percent). The figure for people who sometimes ate/chose fast food, namely several times and once times a week, showed/saw/witnessed a similar trend, rising to 20% and 32.5% respectively in 2006 before falling to around 16% and 27% in turn, in 2013.

The rate of people who ate fast food at restaurants once or twice a month, however, dipped to 25% in 2006 and then jumped dramatically to around 33% in 2013. Moreover, a group of people who consumed a few times a year went up/rose /increased by 2.5% from 2003 to 2006 and remained around 15% in 2013.

206 words

SAMPLE 13

Write a report for a university lecturer describing the information in the graph.

Summarize the information by selecting and reporting the main features, and make comparisons where relevant.

Channel one news viewing figures

(The 11pm news was introduced on 1st May)

The line graph illustrates the number of the audience of Channel One News at different times of the day over a 12-month period.

Overall, the number of viewers at different times, except for the figure/the data for 1 pm (News), experienced/underwent considerable fluctuations during the period shown.

Initially, the figure for viewers at 9.30 pm increased minimally before reaching the peak of just under 4 million in May, but it later declined exponentially to 1 million after 3 months in August. However, a remarkable recovery to 2.5 million in following month/ one month later was recorded, which was followed by a small growth of half a million until the end of the year.

Starting from May, the number of viewers at 11 pm experienced a substantial rise, hit its highest point of 4 million in August, but the figure witnessed a dramatic fall of 3 million in the remaining months (of the year)/ in the remainder of the year. There was a downward trend with fluctuations between 5 and 3 million in the figure for watchers at 6 pm in this year/in the whole/entire year. Meanwhile, the number of people watching the Channel at 1 pm stayed relatively stable/steady during the year, at slightly over 1 million.

207 words

SAMPLE 14

The graph below shows average carbon dioxide (CO2) emissions per person in the United Kingdom, Sweden, Italy and Portugal between 1967 and 2007.

Summarise the information by selecting and reporting the main features, and make comparisons where relevant.

Source: https://baysideielts.wordpress.com/2017/05/25/task-1-line-graph/

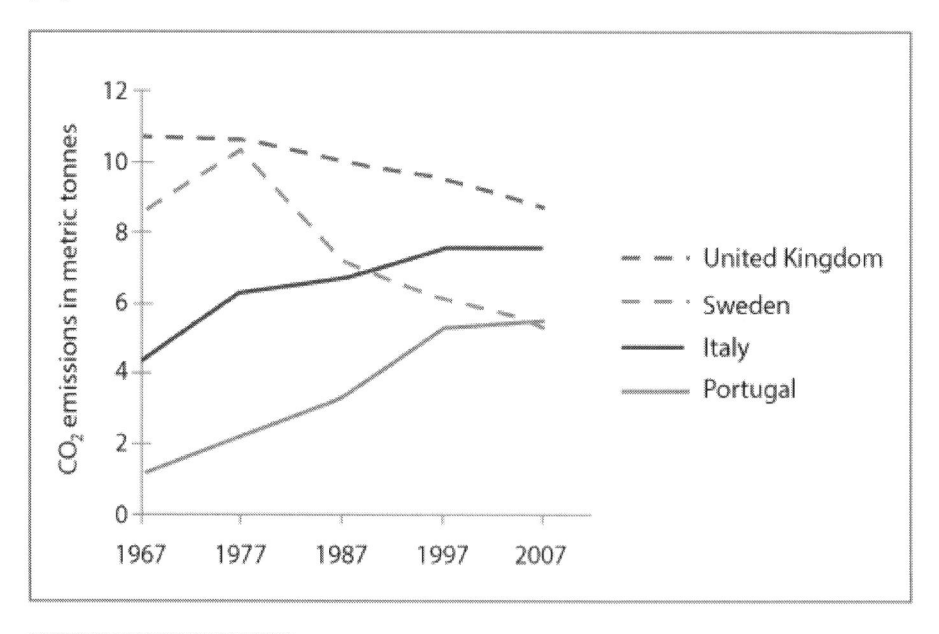

<u>**MODEL ANSWER 1:**</u>

The line graph illustrates the average number of carbon dioxide which was emitted by each resident in four different countries from 1967 to 2007.

Overall, there was a downward trend in the United Kingdom and Sweden, which reversed the trend of two other nations. While the emission of carbon dioxide in the UK always stayed at the highest figure, Portuguese people produced the lowest carbon dioxide rate over a period of 40 years.

To be more specific, in the 1967-1977period, the average amount of carbon dioxide in the UK remained relatively constant, at about 11 metric tonnes, whereas the figures for Sweden, Italy, and Portugal increased moderately to around 10.5, 6.5 and 2.5 metric tonnes, respectively.

Between 1997 and 2007, British saw a slight decrease in the amount of carbon dioxide, at about 2 metric tonnes. Likewise, there was a dramatic decline in the amount of carbon dioxide on average in Sweden from approximately 10.5 metric tonnes to just above 5 metric tonnes, a drop of around 5.5 metric tonnes during 30 years. By contrast, at the end of this period, the Italian sent out the average amount of carbon dioxide with 1 metric tonnes more than they did in 1977. Although the emission of carbon dioxide in Portugal in 2007 reached the highest point at over 5 metric tonnes, this number was the lowest in comparison with the United Kingdom and Italy in the final year.

220 words

MODEL ANSWER 2:

The chart surveys the average amount of carbon dioxide emitted by a person in five different European countries from 1967 to 2007.

Overall, while the amount of CO2 emissions in Sweden and UK were downward, those figures for Italy and Portugal became significant. After 40 years, however, UK still emitted the largest amount of CO2 and despite the remarkable increase, Portugal had the smallest amount of emissions.

On the one hand, in the initial year, the figure for the UK was about 11 metric tonnes of CO2 emissions which was approximately 7 metric tonnes more than that of Italy. However, the amount of emissions in the UK plunged gradually to around 8.5 metric tonnes by 2007. Meanwhile, the figure for Italy leaped remarkably by about 3.8 metric tonnes in 1997 and then levelled off throughout the last ten years.

On the other hand, the figure for Sweden was about 8.2 metric tonnes compared to 1.8 metric tonnes of CO2 released in Portugal in 1967. In the next twelve years, the amount of emissions in Sweden peaked at about 10.5 metric tonnes and then plummeted dramatically to over 6 metric tonnes by 2007. However, regarding Portuguese figure, there was an augment in the amount of emissions in this country which was as same level as Swedish figure in 2007.

218 words

SAMPLE 15

The chart below shows what science graduates from Sometown University after graduating.

Summarise the information by selecting and reporting the main comparisons where relevant.

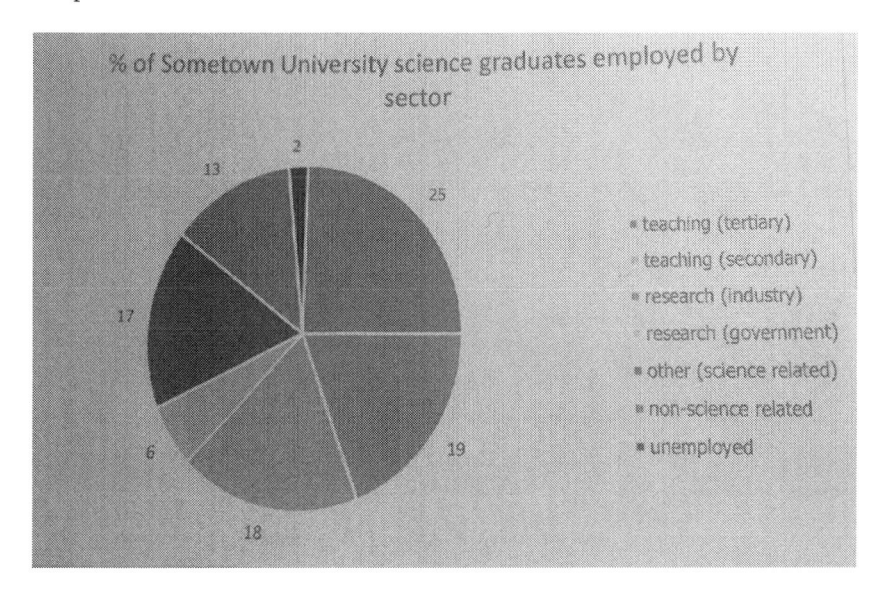

The pie chart compares the percentage of job opportunity of graduates who have studied Science in Sometown University after a year of finishing the school.

Overall, most of the science graduates had/ were able to seek a job that related to their study, whereas just a small amount/ number of students after graduation were become unemployed as well as having a job that was not their specialization.

Teaching was the most common choice for graduates. This accounted for nearly a half of the total, with a quarter of graduate students worked at the universities or college and nearly 20% worked with secondary-school students. In terms of research, 18% of graduate students preferred working in the industry instead of government (6%), tripled than those shown in the others.

35

In contrast/ by contrast, the figures for University leavers who worked in both non-science and science-related job were 17% and 13% respectively. While most of the students who graduated from Sometown University found a job, a small percentage of just only 2% graduates was unemployment after a year of leaving the higher-education.

179 words

SAMPLE 16

The graph shows the income of four cafes in New York in last year.

Summarize the information by selecting and reporting the main features, and make a comparison where relevant.

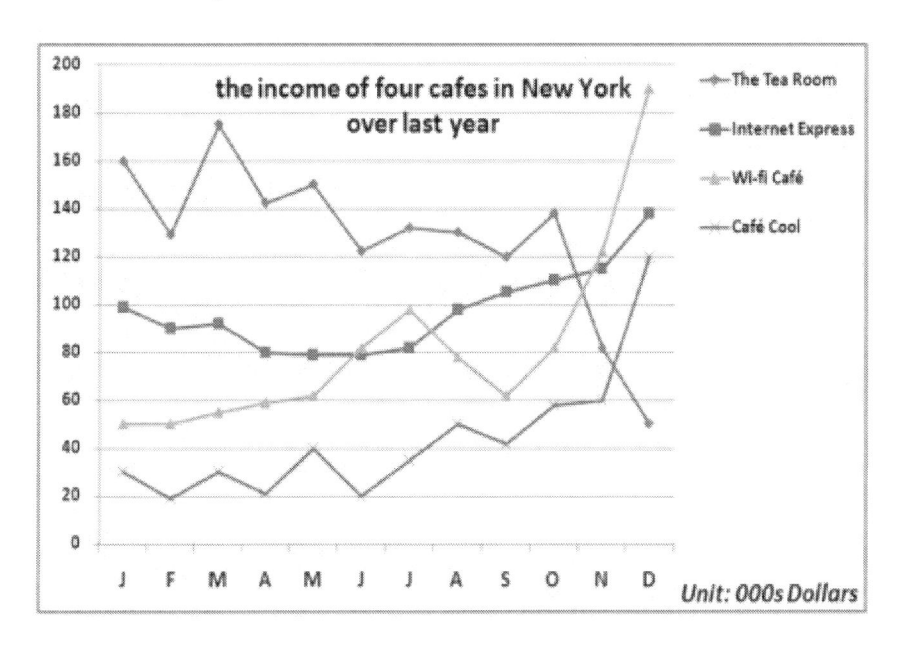

MODEL ANSWER 1:

The line graph illustrates/ compares the income trends of four cafes in the past year.

Overall, the figures for sales of almost all cafes experienced a fluctuating increase except for the Tea Room.

Regarding the Tea Room, the figure fluctuated wildly and then dropped sharply in winter, falling significantly from almost $160,000 to just under $50,000 in December.

On the other hand, the income of the Cafe Cool from lowest sales about $30,000 rocketed suddenly. By contrast, there was a sudden increase in the percentage of the Café Cool from around $30,000 to $120,000 in the last month of the year. Furthermore, the income for both Internet Express and the Wifi Cafe also ended the year up. The former experienced a gradual fall to June of Internet Express, also Wifi Cafe in September. But after that, The Internet Express and Wifi Cafe had sales up more or less to $100,000 and $190,000.

152 words

MODEL ANSWER 2:

The line graph compares four different cafes in New York in terms of monthly earnings in the previous year.

Overall, the three cafes, namely internet Express, Wi-fi Café and Café Cool, saw an upward trend in sales at varying degrees, while The Tea Room's income, albeit at the highest level for almost the whole year, experienced a decrease over the period.

Earnings for The Tea Room was the largest at the beginning of the year, at 160,000$ in January, and remained above any other's until November, when Internet Express and Wi-fi Café respectively overtook its position. In the last two months, the Tea Room's sales fell suddenly from $135,000 in October to as low as $50,000 in December, ending the year with the lowest level.

In January, Internet Express's revenue came second, at about $95,000, which was almost twice as much as that of Wi-fi Café, at approximately $50,000. However, the latter witnessed a higher increase in sales over the next eleven months, reaching a peak of around $190,000 in December, followed by the former, at $135,000. Finally, Café Cool commencing the year with the modest sales of only $30,000 and continuing with a steady rise until November, its sales then rocketed to $120,000 in December.

206 words

SAMPLE 17

The diagrams below show the stages and equipment used in the cement-making process, and how cement is used to produce concrete for building purposes.

Summarize the information by selecting and reporting the main features, and make comparisons where relevant.

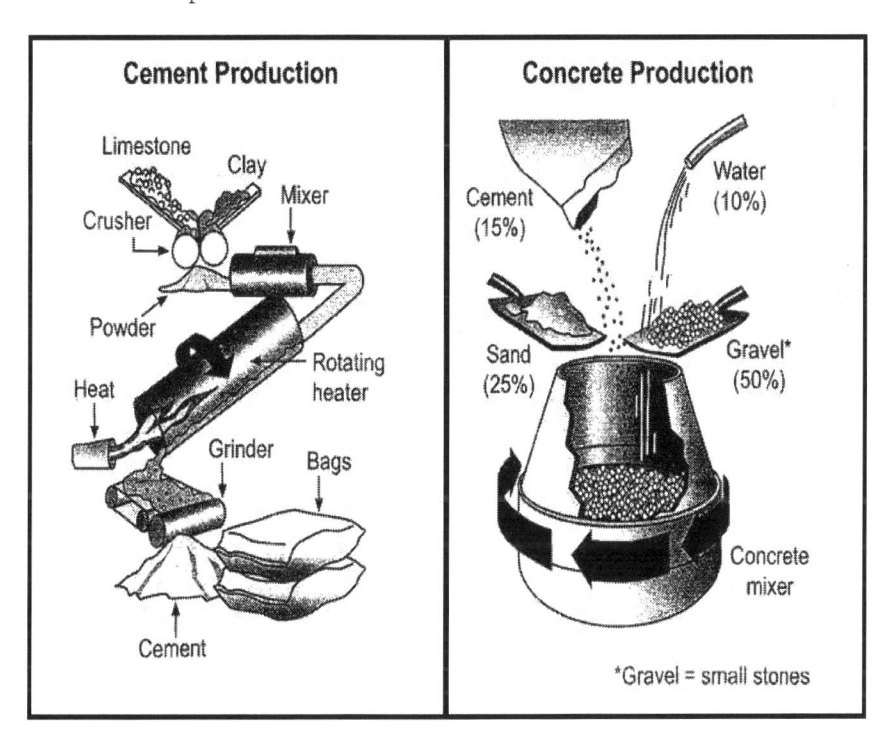

MODEL ANSWER 1:

The two diagrams illustrate the steps and equipment are involved in the cement-making process and how to use cement in the concrete production for building purposes.

It is clear that cement is a combination of limestone and clay which have to go through several stages, beginning with crushing and ending in packaging. Besides, cement is one of four main ingredients to make concrete.

In cement production, limestone and clay are crushed on the first step.

Afterward, these powders are mixed and transferred to the rotating heater at which they are heated directly by fire. Finally, they are ground to produce completed cement, which is packaged in bags.

In the concrete-producing process, cement is combined with 3 other ingredients. Gravel is the largest contribution, at 50%, doubled the figure for sand (25%). Cement contributes only 15%, followed closely by water, at 10%. At the last stage, all four ingredients are combined by a concrete mixture to become finished concrete.

158 words

MODEL ANSWER 2:

The diagrams depict the steps and required tools in the process of making cement, and concrete.

The process of producing cement includes 5 stages, starting from crushing the raw material to packing the final product. And concrete production involves 4 different ingredients.

At first, limestone and clay, which is the raw material used to make cement, is crushed in powder form and mixed in a mixer. And after that, the mixed powder is transferred into a rotating heater, in which the mix is burnt before being put into a grinder. After the mix is ground, it turns into cement. At the end of the process, the cement is stuffed into individual bags.

There are 4 different materials needed to create concrete. Gravel, which is also known as small stones, constitutes half of concrete. Other ingredients include sand (25%), cement (15%) and water (10%). The concrete is produced by mixing all the ingredients together in a concrete mixer.

157 words

SAMPLE 18

A survey conducted for the places in which people gain access to the Internet from 1998 to 2004.

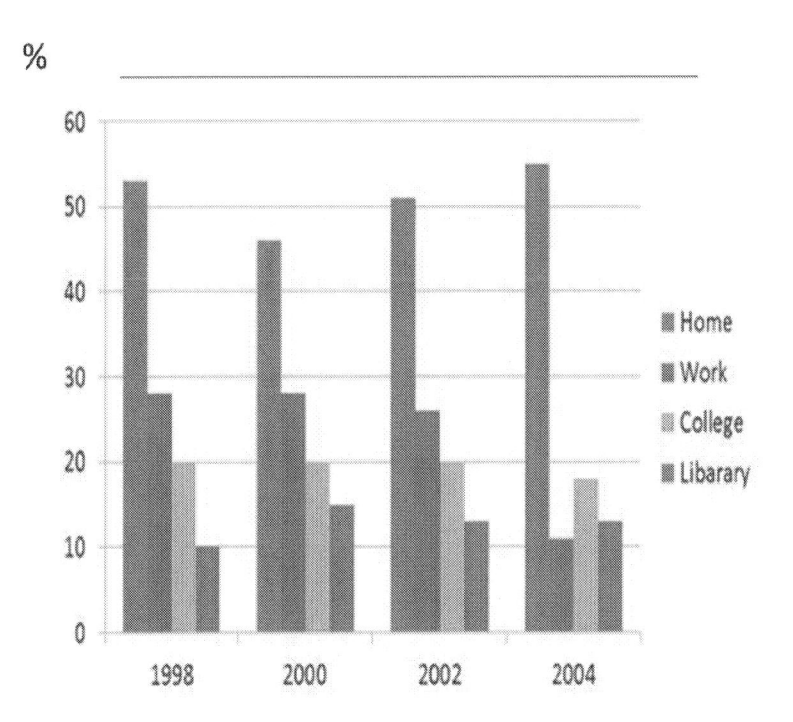

MODEL ANSWER 1:

The bar chart provides information on different locations where people connect to the Internet between 1998 and 2004.

Overall, the proportion of connectors at home and in the library remained relatively unchanged over the period while there was a downward trend in that at work and college. In addition, home by far was recorded to be the most popular place for getting online.

In 1998, more than a half of users gained access to the Internet from their house, which was almost double in comparison to its follower – connectors at work with about 27%. The number of citizens accessing the Internet at college constituted precisely 20%, whereas only 10% was shown to get a connection in the library.

In 2004, the home still maintained as the most common place to access the Internet with approximately 54% after falling moderately by nearly 10% in 2000. On the other hand, the library saw an increase to around 15% of connectors in 2000 before decreasing slightly to around 12% in 2002 and holding steady in 2004. The percentage of users connecting to the Internet at college, which stabilized in the first four years, declined marginally in 2004 to nearly 17%. At the end of the period, this figure at work became the smallest with exactly 10% after going down sharply since 2002.

219 words

MODEL ANSWER 2:

The bar chart illustrates the proportion of different places accessing the Internet from 1998 to 2004.

Overall, the rates of Internet users gaining access to the Internet at home increased during the period of time, while those of people getting online at work and colleges decreased. Meanwhile, the number of ones accessed at library fluctuated.

From 1998 to 2004, the choices of gaining access at home still ranked the first with the maximum point nearly 55% in 2014, which was about 10% higher than in 2000. By contrast, the percentage of gaining Internet access at work decreased significantly, from about 28% in 1998 to nearly 10% in 2010.

In the same period, the proportion of accessing the Internet at colleges had a slight decrease about 2%, from 20% to 18%. By contrast, access in the library experienced a fluctuation with the maximum point about 15% in 2000.

151 words

SAMPLE 19

The graph below shows the unemployment rates in the US and Japan between March 1993 and March 1999. Write a report for a university lecturer describing the information shown below.

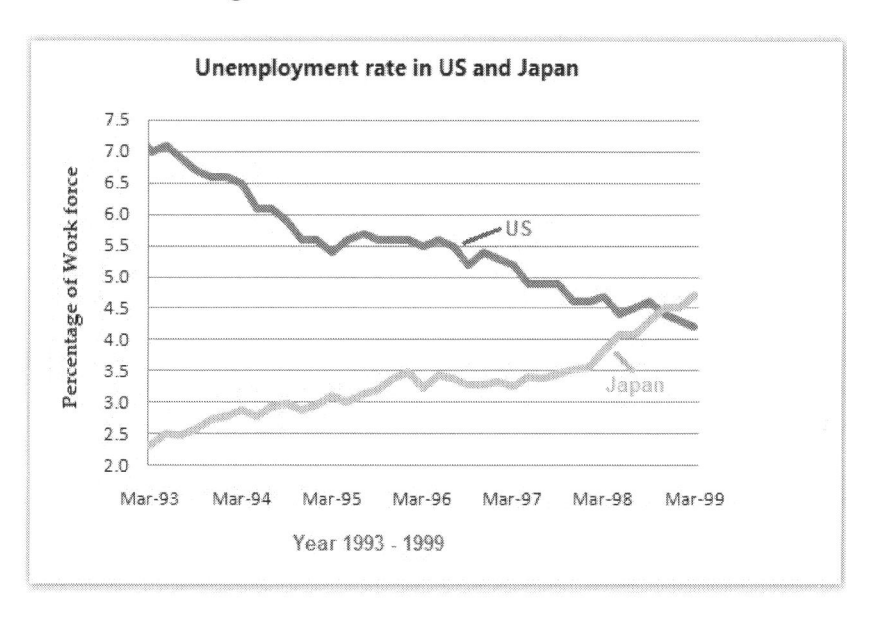

MODEL ANSWER 1:

The given line graph compares the percentages of unemployed people in the USA and in Japan and how these rates changed from March 1993 to March 1999.

Overall, whilst the unemployment rate in America decreased, the figure for Japan increased over the period of 6 years. Additionally, the percentage of the unemployed workforce of the USA in most years was higher than that of Japan.

In March 1993, the USA's unemployment rate stayed at a high level, 7%. The figure, however, began dropping slowly since March 1993 to 5% in the year 1996. Throughout the remainder of the period, there was a slight fluctuation around 5% in the unemployment rate in America.

Regarding the unemployed proportion in Japan, in March 1993, it started at 2.5% mark, which was one-third of that in the USA. However, the Japan's unemployment rate grew to approximately 4.5% by 1996. After that, the ratio of unemployed workforce in Japan kept rising and reached a peak of 5.1% in 1998, before falling negligibly to 5% in 1999.

171 words

MODEL ANSWER 2:

The line chart illustrates the percentage of unemployed people in two different countries namely the US and Japan over a 6-year period from March 1993 to March 1999.

Overall, there was an inverse trend/tendency/pattern between the unemployment rates of the two countries with an upward pattern for Japan and downward for the US. As shown by the graph, the gap between the 2 lines was being narrowed by the time.

Starting at the peak of 7%, the proportion of unemployed people in the US went through a period of sharp fluctuations from March 1993 to March 1996. And the trend was obviously downward. In the following years, the figures for the US hovered around 5% before standing at the same level of Japan in March 1999.

Over the same period, Japan's unemployment rate went up steadily from the lowest point of 2.5% in March 1993, although there were minor ups and downs in the percentage of the unemployed workforce. From March 1996 to the end of 1997, the figures for Japan leveled off at nearly 4.5%, except for a sharp dip to just under 4% in the end of 1996. From 1998 on, the rate of unemployed people in Japan soared to the highest point throughout the period of just over 5% before stabilizing at this level until the end of the 6-year period.

219 words

MODEL ANSWER 3:

The graph reveals the level of unemployment in two specific countries, the United State and Japan through a 7-year-period, from 1993 to 1999.

Overall, there was a complete contrast in the pattern of the two nations, with a downward trend in the US and an increasing rate of unemployed labours in Japan.

Starting from 7% in the beginning of 1993, the level of unemployed workforce in the USA experienced a constant decrease and hit slightly below 5.5% in 1995. Following that was a quite stable year in which the rate remained at somewhere between 5.5% and 6%. From 1996 and afterward, the rate of unemployment continued declining steadily and ended up at just above 4% in 1999.

Japan, on the contrary, witnessed a significant rise in the proportion of unemployment. From just below 2.5% in 1993, the rate grew ceaselessly to reach 3.5% in 1998 before surging up to above 4.5% in 1999, making it almost double the percentage seen in the beginning of the period. It is interesting to note that between 1998 and 1999, the percentage of labours that were out of work in the two countries was equal to 4.5%, however, in the end, the rate in Japan outweighed its counterpart.

204 words

SAMPLE 20

The line graph below shows the percentage of tourists to England who visited four different attractions in Brighton.

Summarise the information by selecting and reporting the main features, and make comparisons where relevant.

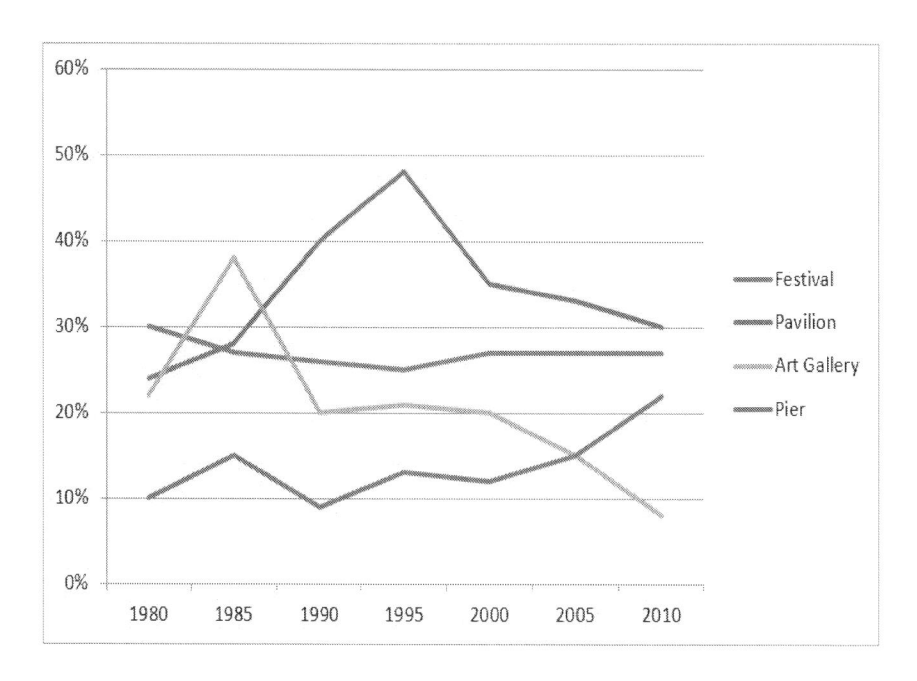

MODEL ANSWER 1:

The line graph compares the proportion of people to England visiting four various attractions in Brighton over a period of 30 years.

Overall, art gallery experienced the fast decline in the percentage of tourists to England over the period shown. In addition, while the numbers of visitors to festival and art gallery decreased, the figures for Pavilion and Pier increased.

In 1980, Festival was the most popular attractions, at about 30% of visitors. While the proportions of tourists travelling to Pavilion and Art Gallery were nearly similar, at 24% and 21% respectively, only 10% of tourists visited Pier, which was much lower compared to the other three attractions. In the following 15 years, Pavilion witnessed a dramatic growth and reached a peak of just below 50% of visitors- the highest figure recorded on the line graph.

In Pavilion, after increasing significantly in the percentage of tourists in 1995, its figure declined suddenly to just over 30% in 2010. While the proportion of visitors to Festival remained relatively stable over the 30-year period, Art Gallery's figure saw a significant fall to about 8% in 2010. By contrast, there was a noticeable rise in the percentage of visitors to Pier with over 20%.

201 words

MODEL ANSWER 2:

A glance at the graph provided reveals the proportion of visitors who came to see four certain Brighton tourist attractions over a given period.

It is evident that in 1980 and in 2010, Pavilion and Festival attracted more people than the other two.

It is apparent from the information supplied that the ratio of tourist coming to Art Gallery increased exponentially over a ten-year period and reached the peak at approximately 39 percent in 1985. This was followed by a period of dramatic decline to the bottom at less than 10 percent in 2010. In a similar pattern development, the proportion of visitors to Pavilion soared from 24 percent in 1980 to peak at 48 percent in 1995. Since then, the percentage saw a sharp fall to 35 percent in 2000, and it continued to steadily lose another 5 percent over the next ten years.

The proportion of tourists to Pier experienced high and low over the same time period; however, it was always lower than the percentage of tourists to other three attractions. Not until 2005 did the Pier rise above the Art Gallery to become the third popular tourist attraction in Brighton. Meanwhile, the ratio of tourists visiting Festival dipped under 30 percent since 1980 and reached a plateau ever since.

213 words

SAMPLE 21

The graph shows Underground Station Passenger Numbers in London.

Summarise the information by selecting and reporting the main features, and make comparisons where relevant.

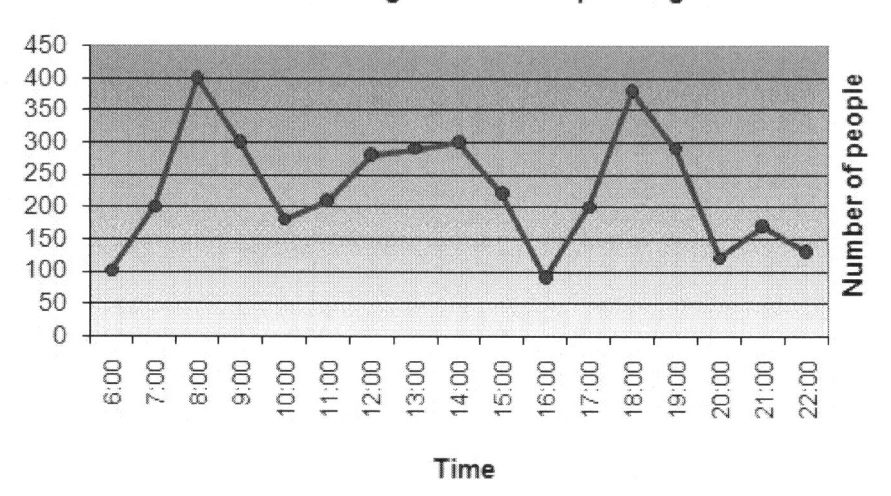

The line graph figures out the number of Underground Station passenger in London regarding different time slots from 6:00 to 22:00.

Overall, the number of people significantly fluctuated over the period of 16 hours in a day. Besides, the rate of office hours was much higher than other time patterns.

From 6:00 to 9:00 and 16:00 to 19:00, the passenger numbers in London fluctuated identically. At 6:00 and 16:00, the number of passengers was 100, but it increased steeply to 200 for an hour, at 7:00 and 17:00 respectively. After that, it continued to ramp up to the highest volume at 8:00 and at 18:00 with around 400 passengers before falling down to around 200 passengers at 9:00. There were a little bit lower passengers at 20:00, approximately 145.

From 9:00 to 16:00, the number of passengers kept changed gradually, started around 190 at 9:00. In the following time slots, it increased sharply and reached 300 passengers at 14:00. The number was down about 200 and spot at 100 passengers at 16:00. Also, the trend in the period of 20:00 to 22:00 remained the same. In particular, it slightly changed from 175 at 21:00 to 145 at 22:00, and made a decline in the number of passengers to 145 at the end of the line.

215 words

SAMPLE 22

The diagrams below give information on transport and car use in Edmonton.

Summarise the information by selecting and reporting the main features, and make comparisons where relevant.

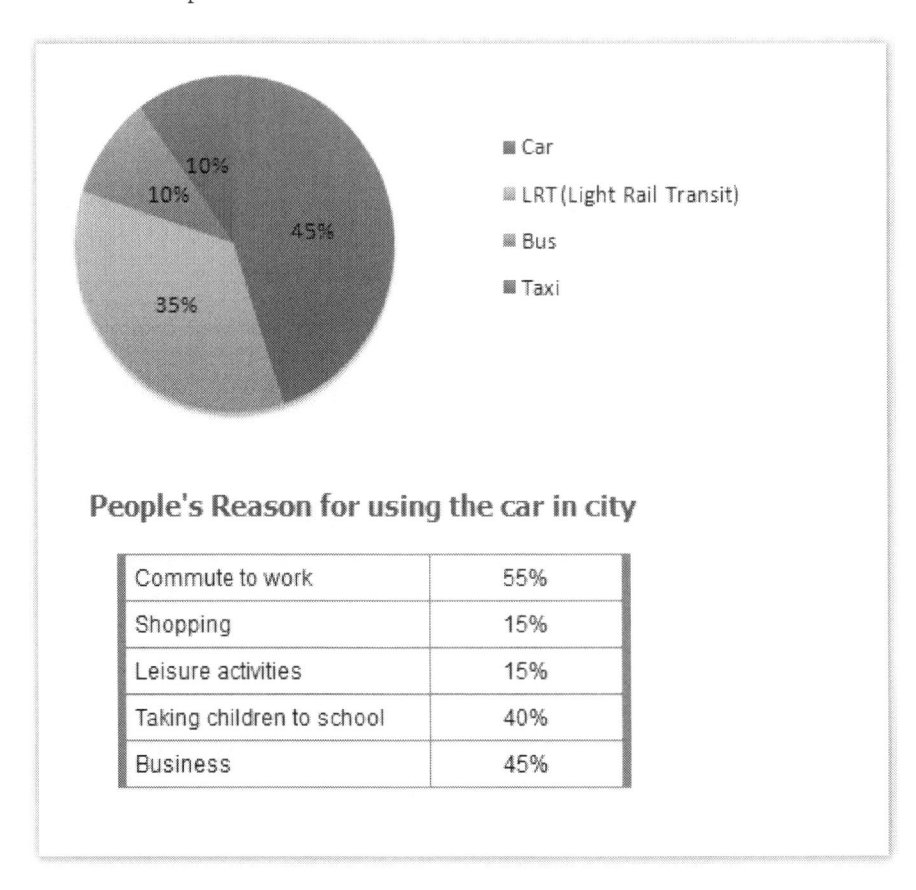

People's Reason for using the car in city

Commute to work	55%
Shopping	15%
Leisure activities	15%
Taking children to school	40%
Business	45%

The pie chart illustrates the proportion of means of transportation use in Edmonton, whereas the table explains different reasons why people need cars in the city.

Overall, it can clearly be seen that car takes the lion's share among all given transportation forms. This is because cars seem to be the most convenient road vehicles that can facilitate people to get to work, complete their business trips or drop their children to school.

According to the pie chart, it is noticeable that car is widely preferred in Edmonton with 45% usage of all transportation forms available. The second largest choice is Light Rail Transit with 35%, indicating that 3 out of 10 Edmonton townsmen travel by train. By contrast, bus and taxi equally share moderate proportions of 10% each, being the least used vehicles in the list.

With regards to the purpose of car utility, 55% people respond that cars serve the purpose of travelling to work. Business and taking children to school rank next, with 45% and 40% respectively. By contrast, only 15% people in Edmonton report that they use cars for shopping or leisure activities.

187 words

SAMPLE 23

The diagrams show a structure that is used to generate electricity from wave power.

Summarise the information by selecting and reporting the main features, and make comparisons where relevant.

Generating electricity from sea waves

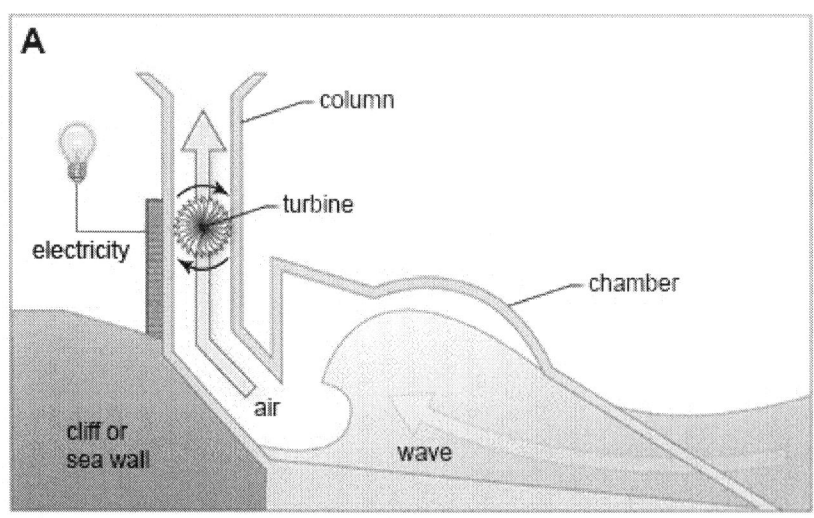

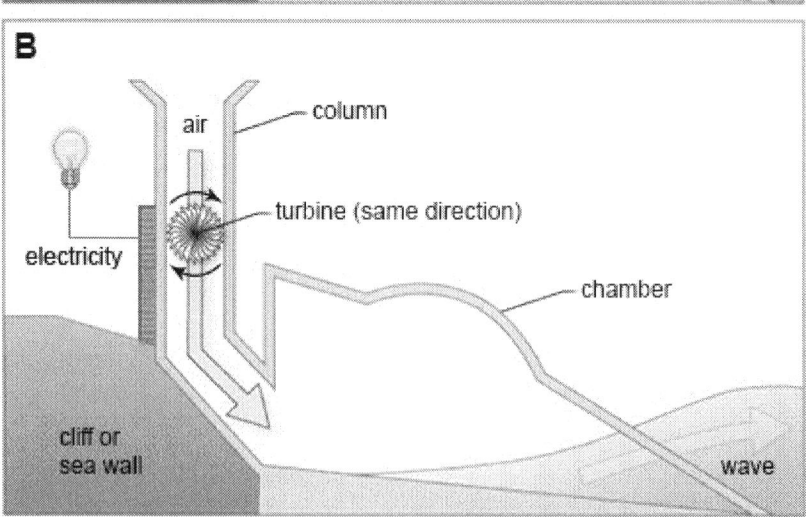

MODEL ANSWER 1:

The given figures illustrate how electricity is generated from taking advantage of sea waves.

Overall, the process involves a structure constructed on a cliff or sea wall. In particular, this structure consists of a large chamber which has one side opening to the sea while the other leads to a vertical column opening to the atmosphere. A turbine is installed inside the column in order to create the electricity in two phases different situations.

The first diagram represents phase one the 1st situation occurring when the sea wave rises into the chamber and applies pressure on the air inside the system, forces forcing it to go through the turbine. This move encourages the turbine to rotate, from which electricity is generated.

The second diagram indicates the next phase 2nd situation of the process when the wave falls. As the water level declines, the air from outside is sucked back in the column through the turbine. As a consequence, electricity is constantly created. Remarkably, the turbine always rotates in one direction regardless of the direction of the air flow.

178 words

MODEL ANSWER 2:

The diagrams illustrate how electricity is produced in two cases when sea waves rise and fall.

Overall, the key difference between the diagrams is that they show the opposite ways of air contribution. In either case, there is the same structure to create electricity, which is installed on the side of a cliff or sea wall. This structure consists of a large chamber. One end is open to the sea, and the other leads into a vertical column, which is open to the atmosphere.

The first diagram indicates that when a wave approaches the device, water is forced into the chamber, and then applying pressure on the air within the column. This air escapes to atmosphere through the turbine, which is placed inside the column, thereby producing electricity.

When the level of seawater falls, as shown in the second diagram, the air from outside the column is sucked back in. In this case, with the same direction and production mechanism of the turbine, electricity continues to be generated.

168 words

SAMPLE 24

The bar chart below shows the employment of all male and female workers by occupation in the UK in the year 2005.

Summarize the information by selecting and reporting the main features, and make comparisons where relevant.

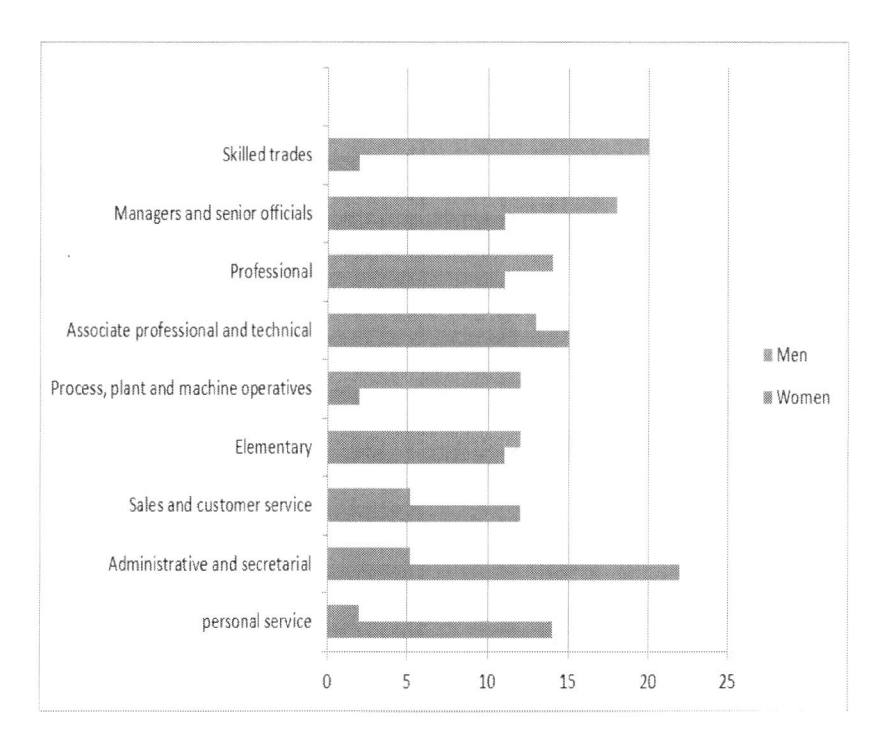

The chart shows data about the proportion of employees in both genders by professions in the UK in 2005.

Overall, there are many differences in choosing a career of men and women workers. It is clear that women tend to work in service occupations, while men prefer to perform managerial or professional jobs.

In 2005, the proportion of females working in administrative and secretarial position was highest, at about 22%, compared to only over 5% of men doing in this area as well as customer service. Likewise, personal service occupations were attracting more women than men, with almost 15% of women. Men, on the other hand, preferred to work in skilled trades. This figure was exactly 20%, while only about 2% of women joining in this field. Also, only approximately 11% of female employees worked in managers and senior officials, as well as professional jobs, these figures for men, were roughly 17% and 14%, respectively.

The percentage of females who associated with professional and technical trades was precisely 15%, which was a bit higher than male, a difference of 2%. There were a similar proportion of both genders in elementary jobs with the average about 11%. However, in terms of process, plant and machine operatives, men enjoyed working in this field much more than women with 12%.

217 words

SAMPLE 25

The charts below show the results of a survey of adult education. The first chart shows the reasons why adults decide to study. The pie chart shows how people think the costs of adult education should be shared.

Write a report for a university lecturer, describing the information shown below. You should write at least 150 words.

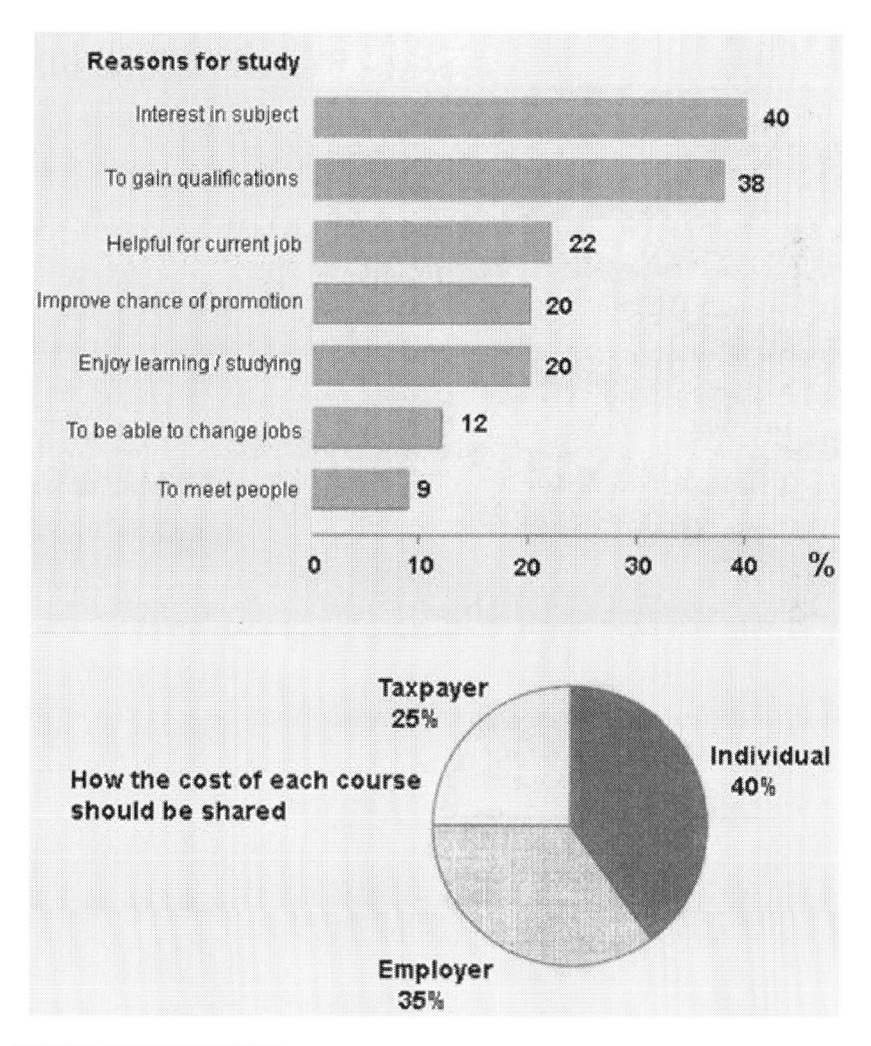

MODEL ANSWER 1:

The charts illustrate data on different reasons for adult's further study and the people who are believed to be responsible for the tuition.

Overall, being interested in subject and getting qualifications are two major reasons for further study. Besides, the majority of tuition fees are thought to be paid by individuals.

It can be seen from the first chart that the largest proportion of the adults continuing their study because of their favor of the subject and the qualifications they will obtain, at 40% and 38% respectively. By contrast, the smallest percentage runs into the ability to change the jobs and making acquaintance, 12% for the former and only 9% for the later. The three remained reasons share the similar figures which are mostly a half of the first one, 22% for helpful for the current job and each 20% for promotion and study enjoyment.

It can be seen from the second chart that individuals themselves have to pay the most for their study, at 40% of the costs. However, the amount of money that employers and taxpayers are believed to be responsible for is slightly lower, 35% and 25% respectively.

191 words

MODEL ANSWER 2:

The first chart illustrates some reasons for adults' academic decisions, and the second chart reveals participants' perception on how to share the cost of adult education.

It is clear that subject interest accounted for the largest proportion of academic decisions while the demand for people meeting remained as the least choice. Out of three categories of course price sharing, individual responsibility in academic fee payment had the highest percentage.

The figure for subject attractiveness was highest with 40% [registered the greatest proportion of 40%] and qualification achievement nearly stood at that amount with 38%. While the data for meeting people and job alteration ability was at around one-fourth of that amount, 9% and 12% respectively, benefits for current jobs, promotion improvement and learning interest remained at around one half of that amount.

It can be seen that there was not much difference between the three groups of the cost-sharing survey. Although individual was most likely to pay for their own studying with the percentage of a substantial 40%, employer and taxpayer were not far different from that number with an insignificant 35% and an appreciable 25% respectively.

187 words

SAMPLE 26

The table below gives information about changes in modes of travel in England between 1985 and 2000.

Summarize the information by selecting and reporting the main features, and make comparisons where relevant.

	1985	2000
Walking	255	237
Bicycle	51	41
Car	3199	4806
Local bus	429	274
Local distance bus	54	124
Train	239	366
Taxi	13	42
Other	450	585
All modes	4740	6475

The table illustrates the proportion of miles travelled by a British person in terms of 8 kinds of transportation in Britain over two separate years, 1985 and 2000.

Overall, car accounted for the greatest number of miles in both years. Additionally, it is obvious that there was a reduction in the figure for miles seen in walking, bicycle, local bus whereas car, local distance bus, train, taxi and other means of transportation witnessed an increase.

In 1985, car was the primary use of commuting by British citizen at precisely 3155 miles, after 15 years, its figure experienced a significant growth by 1607 miles to reach 4806 miles, which was also the highest proportion in 2000. Over the period of 15 years, there was a dramatic increase in the number of miles travelled by local distance bus, from 54 miles to 124 miles in 1985 and 2000 respectively. During the 15-year period, train saw a noticeable increase, climbing to 366 miles in 2000. Taxi covered for exactly 13 miles in 1985, however, after 15 years, its section went up dramatically to 42 miles, which was the second position in 2000. Also, there was an increase in the number of miles seen in other kinds of transport of 135 miles, rising to 585 miles in 2000.

In the figure for miles commuted by walking, its portion experienced a slight decrease, which fell to 237 miles in 2000 from 255 miles in the year 1985. Accounting for only 51 miles in 1985, there were 10 miles fall over the 15-year period to 41 miles, remaining as the lowest point in 2000. Over the same period shown, local bus saw a reduction, from 429 miles to 274 miles in 1985 and 2000 respectively.

220 words

SAMPLE 27

The line graph compares the percentage of people in three countries who used the Internet between 1999 and 2009.

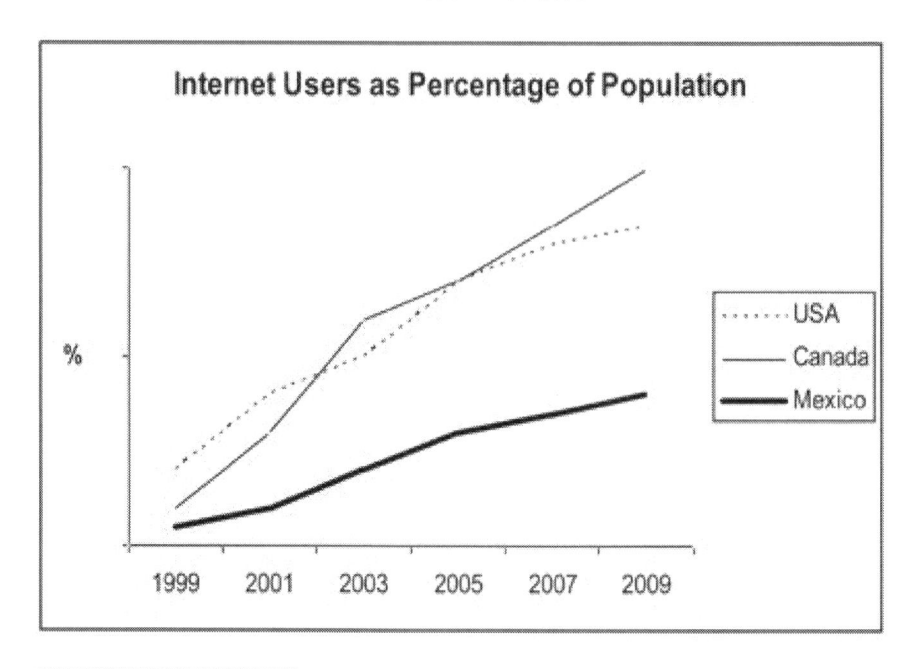

MODEL ANSWER 1:

The line graph compares the percentage of the population who used the internet in the USA, Canada, and Mexico between 1999 and 2009.

Overall, the proportion of internet users in three countries increased over the period of 10 years. Although the three trends were similar in terms of a general growth, the percentage of people who used the internet in Mexico was lower than that in both the USA and Canada.

In the year 1999-2001, internet users as a percentage of the population in three countries rose steadily. The figure for Mexico was lowest, at about 5%. The figures for the USA and Canada were higher, at about 12% and 22% respectively. In 2005, the proportion of people who used the internet grew significantly in both USA and Canada, at around 75%, while the figure for Mexico just reached 30%.

Throughout the remainder of the period, there was a stable increase of internet users of the population in three countries. The figure for Canada was highest at almost 100%. The percentages of the Canada and Mexico were 85% and 40% respectively.

181 words

MODEL ANSWER 2:

The line graph illustrated the figures for residents using the internet in the three countries from 1999 to 2009.

Overall, the three countries saw an increase in internet usage over a 10 year-period. The percentage of the population in the USA and Canada who had access to the Internet was much larger than that in Mexico.

In 1999, the proportion of Mexicans who used the internet was lowest, at about 5%. In comparison, the figures for Canadians and Americans were higher, at about 10% and 20% respectively. By the year 2005, the percentage of people having the internet access in both nations, Canada and the USA, reached around 70% while the internet usage in Mexico rose to just over 25%.

By 2009, the majority of people in the USA and Canada used the internet, at about 80% and almost 100% respectively. Meanwhile, a much smaller percentage of Mexicans used the Internet, at only 40%.

155 words

SAMPLE 28

The diagram below shows the typical stages of consumer goods manufacturing, including the process by which information is fed back to earlier stages to enable adjustment.

Write a report for a university lecturer describing the process shown.

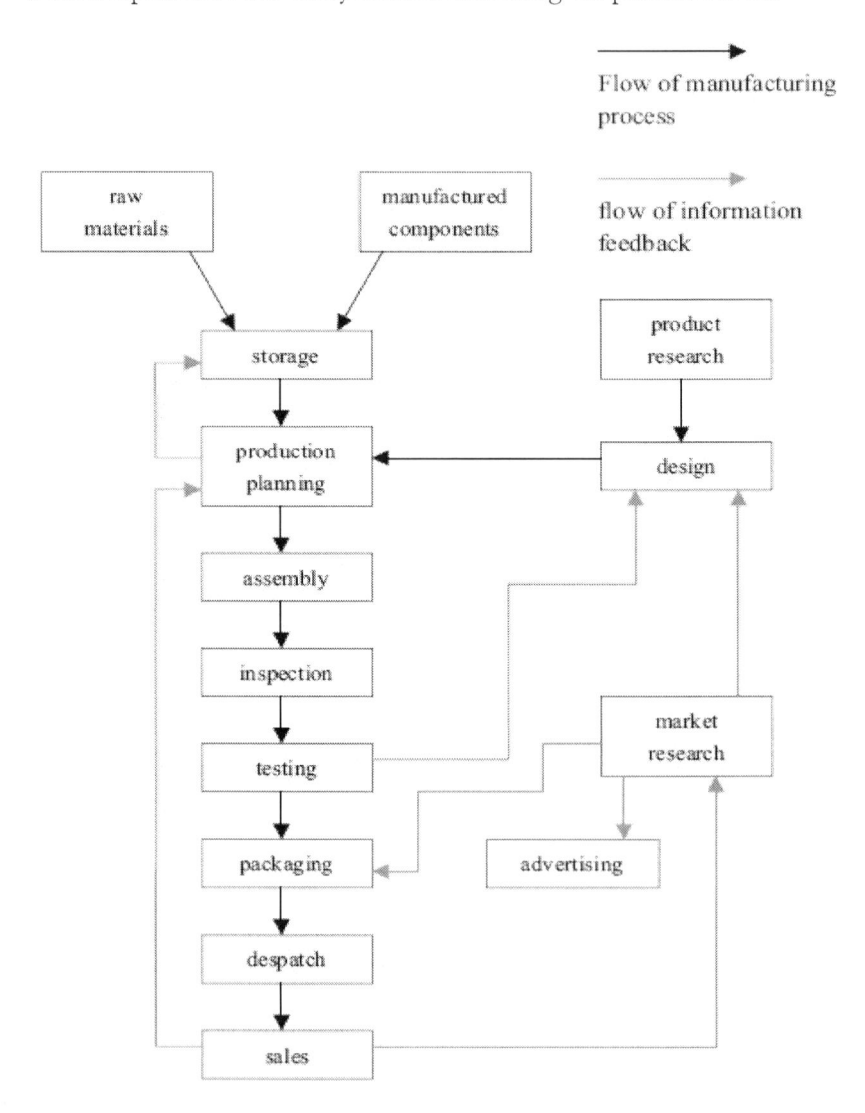

The diagram describes the process in which consumer goods are produced as well as how feedback is transferred to the earlier stage for modification.

Overall, the goods manufacturing is a complex operation chain, which includes two main processes: the flow of producing and flow of the feedback, from the initial storage to the eventual selling.

At the first stage, raw materials and other components are stored. Results from both product and market researches are collected as input for designing. Then, the layout and earlier accumulated elements are used in production planning. Together with this step, feedback is sent to the storage stage.

Next, the process continues with assembly, inspection, and testing stages, sequentially. Feedback from the testing stage is sent back to design stage. If the products are qualified after testing, they, then, are packaged in accordance with information from market research. This information is also used for advertisement. The procedure concludes with dispatch and sale stages.

157 words

SAMPLE 29

The maps below show how the town of Harborne changes from 1936 to 2007. Summarize the information by selecting and reporting the main features, and make comparisons where relevant.

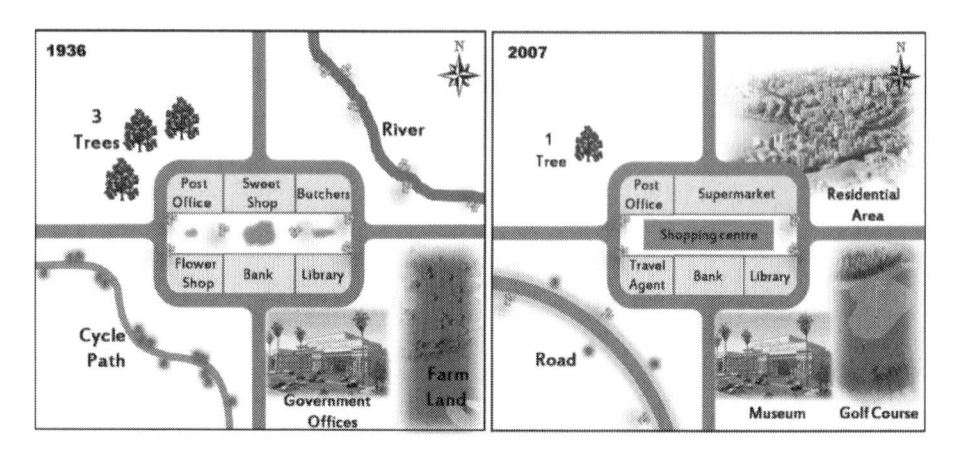

MODEL ANSWER 1:

The maps describe the development of the Harborne town between 1936 and 2007.

Overall, this town transformed significantly. While some of the natural beauties were cut out, the residential area was expanded and more options for shopping and leisure activities became available.

From 1936 to 2007, there were more residents living by the river in the north-east of the town. In this period, a noticeable number of trees in the north-west were chopped down. In the center of Harborne, a new shopping center was constructed. While the post office, bank, and library remained, the sweet shop and butchers were rebuilt into a brand-new supermarket. Opposite the post office, where a flower shop used to be, they built a travel agency.

The cycle path, which was situated in the south-west of the town, was redesigned as a road. In the south-east, the government offices were converted into a museum and a golf course took over the place of an old farmland.

160 words

MODEL ANSWER 2:

The diagrams illustrate the development of Harborne town in 1936 and 2007.

Overall, there was a significant development in town between 1936 and 2007. Most of the natural landscapes were taken away and replaced by extending of a residential zone and variety of options for shopping and entertainment. These significant changes might be due to the effect of industrialization and increasing of populations.

From 1936 to 2007, a number of plants in northeastern fall sharply to one-third. In addition, the beautiful river located in the northwest region was replaced by a large area of the residential zone.

Over 7 decades, locations of the post office, bank and library still stayed the same. However, in 2007, the adjacent to the bank was travel agent instead of the flower shop in 1936. In addition, the area of sweet shop and butchers was redesigned into a supermarket. Additionally, natural cycle path was replaced by modern road in the southeastern part of the city. Opposite to that direction, in the southwest region, the occurrences of museum and golf course replace for the disappear of government offices and farmland, respectively.

185 words

SAMPLE 30

The graph below gives information from a 2008 report about consumption of energy in the USA since 1980 with projections until 2030.

Summarise the information by selecting and reporting the main features, and make comparisons where relevant.

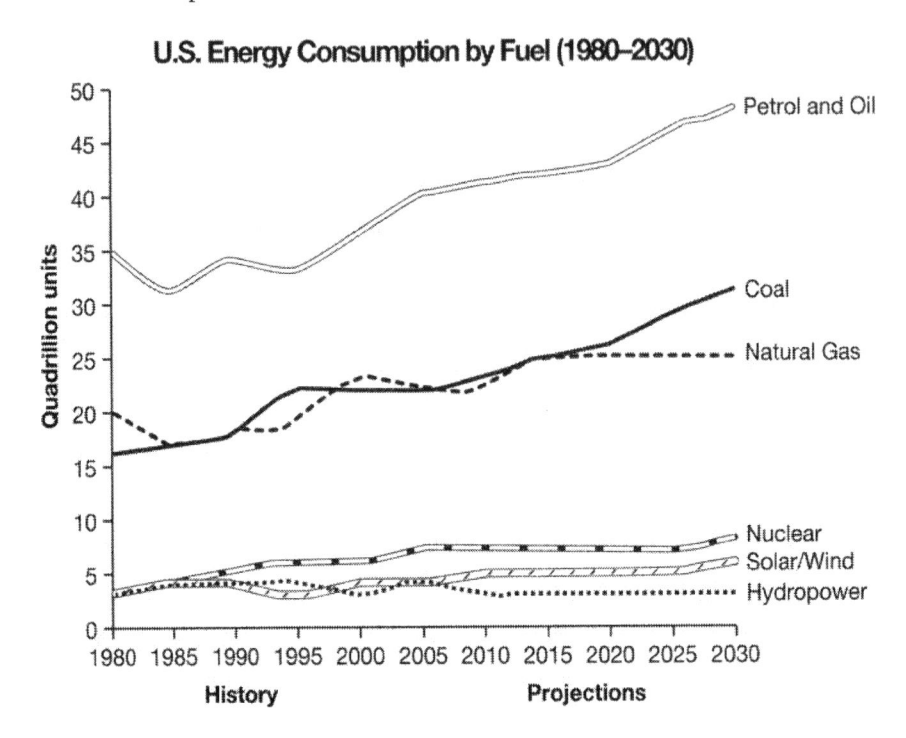

U.S. Energy Consumption by Fuel (1980–2030)

MODEL ANSWER 1:

The line graph shows data about energy consumption in the USA between 1980 and 2030.

Overall, the consumption of Hydropower, Solar/Wind and Nuclear energy remained relatively constant throughout a period of 50 years. While there was a gradual increase in consumption of 5 other kinds of fuel, Petrol and Oil were used the most in both the past and projections for the future.

In 1980, around 35 quadrillions of energy consumed was Petrol and Oil. Natural Gas energy commenced at 20 quadrillions while the figure for Coal energy began at about 16 quadrillions. The 3 other kinds of fuel were consumed at the same figure, which was at around 3 quadrillions in the first year.

The amount of Petro and Oil consumption grow gradually from 1980 to 2030 and is predicted to peak at approximately 50 quadrillions in the final year. The figure for Coal energy rises steadily throughout the period, which will be responsible for around 30 quadrillions in 2030. Likewise, the prediction for Natural Gas energy consumption is at about 25 quadrillions. The trend for Nuclear power, Solar/Wind, and Hydropower doesn't change much throughout the period.

188 words

MODEL ANSWER 2:

The line graph illustrates the changes in consumption of energy in the USA from 1980 with predictions to 2030.

Overall, the use of fuel in American has an upward trend over the period. Petrol and Oil were consumed in the largest amount between 1980 and 2015, and they are forecasted to keep this trend until 2030.

It can be seen from the graph that the consumption of Solar/Wind fluctuated from 1980 to 2010 and then remained stable at 5 quadrillion units before increasing slightly to about 7 quadrillion units in 2030. It was also the case for Hydropower though it was used averagely 2 quadrillion units less than Solar/Wind and was predicted to reach nearly 4 quadrillion units in the last year. Nuclear always saw a gradual growth in utilization during the period, rose from 3 quadrillion units in 1980 to 9 quadrillion units in 2030.

In the first 35 years, the use of Coal jumped at various rates while that of Natural Gas went up and down. At the end of the period, they are believed to reach the relatively high levels (30 and 25 quadrillion units). In terms of Petrol and Oil consumption, there was a slight variation in the early years and a sharp rise to 45 quadrillion units by 2015. It is thought that this figure will approximately reach 50 quadrillion units in 2030.

219 words

SAMPLE 31

The chart below shows the number of travelers using three major airports in New York City between 1995 and 2000.

Summaries the information by selecting and reporting the main features, and make comparisons where relevant.

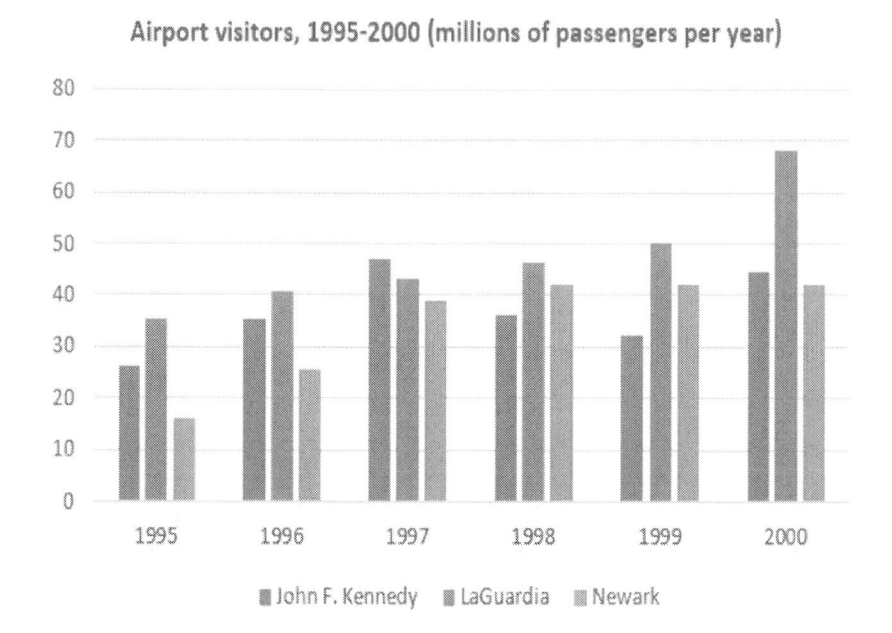

Airport visitors, 1995-2000 (millions of passengers per year)

MODEL ANSWER 1:

The bar graph gives information about the number of tourists using three primary airports in New York City in the period of time from 1995 to 2000.

Overall, both LaGuardia and Newark saw an increase in the number of passengers, with the exception of that at John F. Kennedy.

In 1995, only 15 million travellers used Newark airport, which was 20 million smaller than the number of LaGuardia. These two figures continued to rise in the next three years and reached 42 million and 46 million, respectively. After that, the number of Newark remained constant for the coming years, while that of LaGuardia kept rising and reaching its peak at 68 million, the highest number recorded in the chart.

The number of passengers of John F. Kennedy airport was 26 million in 1995 and climbed gradually to 46 million in 1997. This figure decreased to 36 million in 1998 and 32 million in 1999 and then considerably rose to 44 million in 2000.

163 words

MODEL ANSWER 2:

The bar chart provides information about three major airports in New York in terms of the number of users from 1995 to 2000.

It is noticeable that LaGuardia experienced a gradual increase in the number of visitors using this airport over the period. On the other hand, the figures for John F. Kennedy airport fluctuated variously during the period between 1995 and 2000.

In 1995, the number of travelers served by LaGuardia airport was highest with around 35 million passengers, followed by John F. Kennedy with approximately 26 million people. Later, the figures for LaGuardia climbed steadily and slightly to nearly 42 million users in 1997 while the number of visitors choosing John F. Kennedy soared and reached a peak of around 45 million passengers. In contrast, there was a tripling in the number of passengers of Newark from 15 million in 1995 to nearly 40 million users in 1997 but this airport was by far the lowest point during this period.

In the latter half of the selected period, the figures for LaGuardia rocketed and peak at 70 million people and made LaGuardia become the most popular airport in New York in 2000. On the other hand, the number of visitors using John F. Kennedy dropped minimally before rising considerably in 2000. The figures for Newark remained relatively constant.

219 words

SAMPLE 32

The chart below shows the amount spent on six consumer goods in four European countries.

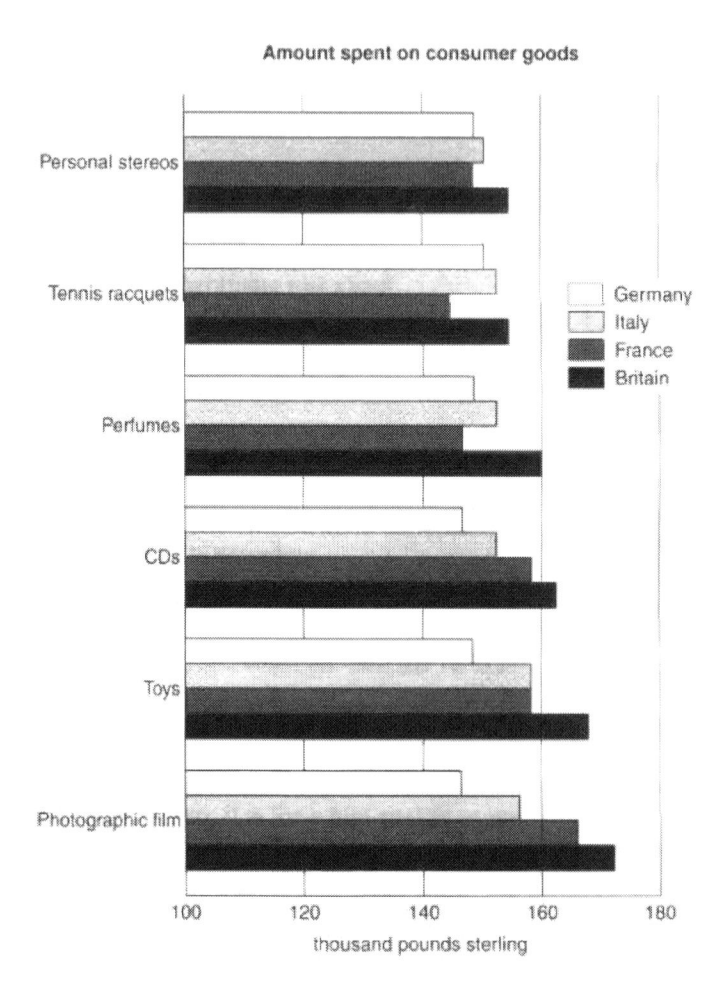

The bar chart compares data on the amount of money that people living in four countries Germany, Italy, France and Britain used to buy six different products.

Overall, it is clear that Britain was by far the country spending the most money on every single item. It is also noted that the one which people tended to buy was photographic film, compared to other kinds of goods.

On the one hand, people in Britain spent about over $170.000 on photographic film which is the highest number amongst four nations, whereas the figure for Germany was just under $150.000 – the lowest overall for all six items. Meanwhile, CDs and Toys were the second most consumed products by people in these separate countries. While there was a similar pattern for Britain and Germany, the amount spent by the other two nations were between $150.000 and $158.000

However, there were some differences in the expense that each country spent on personal stereos, tennis racquets and perfumes. Italians used almost the same amount of money - $150.000 on those items. French, in contrast, spent the least on all three kinds of good.

188 words

SAMPLE 33

The bar chart below shows the percentage of adults of different age groups in the UK who used the Internet every day from 2003-2006.

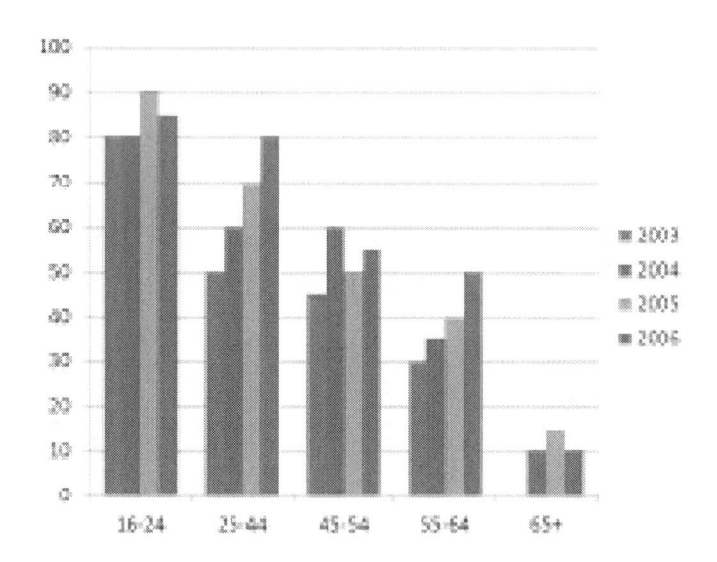

<u>MODEL ANSWER 1:</u>

The bar chart compared the five different age groups of people who accessed the internet on daily basis in the UK between 2003 and 2006.

It is clear that 16-27 age group in the UK accounted for the highest points of the whole graph over the four-year period. Also, aged 25-44 and 55-64 saw the largest rises in Internet users over the same period.

In 2003, the percentage of people from 16-24 age groups was exactly 80%, compared to precisely 50% of people aged 25-44. The figures for the youngest group and aged 25-44 saw only a small increase of a full 10%. In 2006, people accessing the internet from aged 16-24 were by far the highest in terms of users in the UK, and the second one was the older age group, 25-44 age group.

The proportion of Internet users gaining access from three other age groups, 45-54, 55-64, 65 and oversaw a relatively small rise in users between 2003 and 2004 in the UK. In 2005, these age groups used exactly 50%, 40%, and approximately 15% respectively. In2006, the figure for aged 45-54 reached nearly 55%, while 55-to 64-years-old age groups' users figures increased dramatically and the percentage of the oldest age group fluctuated slightly, 65-years-old and over.

210 words

MODEL ANSWER 2:

The diagram highlights the proportion of daily adult Internet users in terms of 5 age groups from 2003 to 2006.

Overall, it is self-evident that the use of internet decreased with age throughout the period. Also notably, 2005 and 2006 witnessed a rise in the percentage of Internet users.

Adults aged less than 25 tended to use the Internet the most. For example, in 2003, around 80% of users were below 25 years old while there were no users aged more than 65. In 2006, though the gap between the 16-24 and 25-44 age group was minor, only 10% of users were recorded to be above 65 years old.

Furthermore, the last 2 years of the period accounted for the highest figure in most age groups. In the youngest group, the percentage figures for the year 2005 and 2006 were 90% and 85%, leaving two remaining years behind. The only exception was among adults aged above 45 and below 54. Starting at 45% in 2003, the figure managed to peak in 2004 at 60%, ending at 55% in 2006.

179 words

SAMPLE 34

The chart below gives information about global population percentages and distribution of wealth by region.

Summarise the information by selecting and reporting the main features, and make comparisons where relevant.

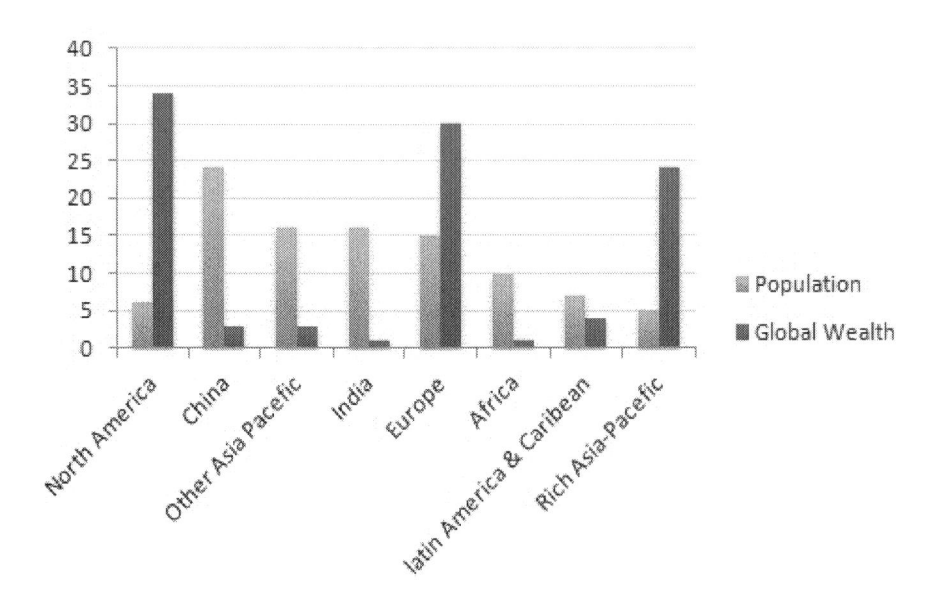

The bar chart compares eight major regions in terms of global population and wealth distribution worldwide.

It is clear from the bar graph that North America has the highest percentage of global wealth distribution, but the second lowest figure for the population. China, on the other hand, has the largest population, but second lowest proportion of distributed wealth.

Looking at the chart in details, global wealth accounts for nearly 35% in North America, compared to 30% in Europe and approximately a quarter in Rich Asia-Pacific. However, the percentages of global population in these regions are quite low, at about 5% for both North America and Rich Asia-Pacific and 15% for Europe, which is half of its proportions of wealth distribution.

In other regions, the figures for population seem to be much higher than those for wealth. 15% of the world population can be noticed in China, while global population accounts for around 15% in Other Asia Pacific region and India. Africa and India have negligible figures for distributed wealth globally, at just 1%, whereas Latin America & Caribean region only makes up 4% of the distribution of wealth worldwide.

189 words

SAMPLE 35

The graph shows oil production capacity for several Gulf countries between 1990 and 2010.

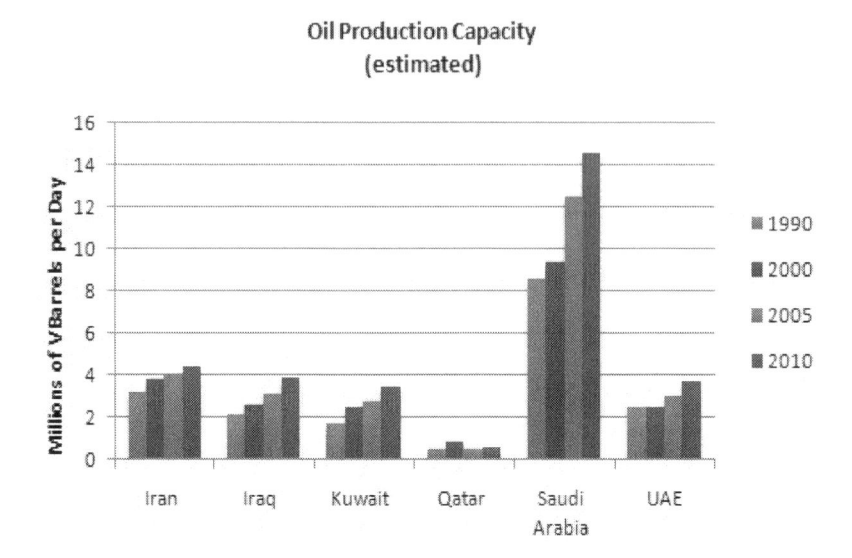

Oil Production Capacity (estimated)

MODEL ANSWER 1:

The graph compares changes in oil production in millions of barrels per day in six Gulf countries over the period from 1990 to 2010.

Overall, it is clear that oil production increased in all countries except for Qatar over the period shown. However, Saudi Arabia experienced the most significant rise and produced the largest amount of oil in each year.

In 1990, Saudi Arabia produced well over 8 million barrels per day, followed by a huge rise by 4 million barrels per day in 2005 before soaring to just above 14 million barrels per day in 2010. In contrast, Qatar was the country with lowest oil production which was stable under 1 million barrels per day over the period.

Oil production capacity in Iran increased gradually from about 3 million barrels per day in 1990 to well over 4 million barrels per day in 2010. Although the production of oil in three countries including Iraq, Kuwait and UAE witnessed a sustainable rise, they still remained under 4 million barrels per day by the year 2010.

175 words

<u>MODEL ANSWER 2:</u>

The provided bar graph illustrates the amount of estimated oil production in six countries starting from 1990 to 2010, measured in millions of barrels per day.

Overall, oil produced in all nations tended to rise over a period of 20 years. In addition, the highest amount of oil production was Saudi Arab, while Qatar was the lowest figure in these countries.

There was a dramatic increase in the oil production capacity in Saudi Arab from slightly over 8 million barrels per day in 1990 to over 14 million barrels per day in the year 2010. In contrast, oil production in Qatar fluctuated and slightly rose throughout the given years with less than 1 million barrels per day.

The other countries saw a stable rise between 1990 and 2010. The oil production in Iran was higher than in the rest of countries with approximately 3 million barrels in 1990 and just over 4 million barrels per day in 2010. Meanwhile, Iraq, Kuwait, and UAE were the places where only around 2 million barrels of oil was produced in 1990 and this figure grew to nearly 4 million barrels per day at the end of this period.

195 words

SAMPLE 36

The charts below show what UK graduate and postgraduate students who did not go into full-time work did after leaving college in 2008.

Summarise the information by selecting and reporting the main features, and make comparisons where relevant.

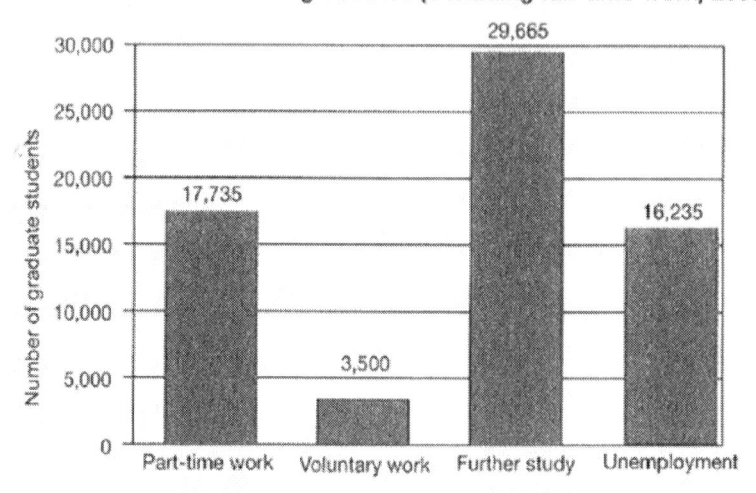

Destination of UK graduates (excluding full-time work) 2008

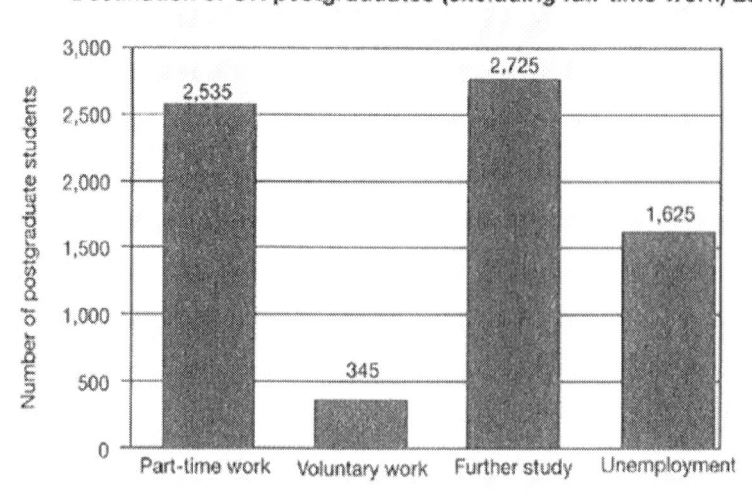

Destination of UK postgraduates (excluding full-time work) 2008

MODEL ANSWER 1:

The charts give information about the destination of UK graduate and postgraduate students with the exception of full-time work after graduation in 2008.

Overall, further study was the unanimous choice for both graduate and postgraduate students, as opposed to the option of minority-voluntary work. Additionally, the numbers of graduate students in four sectors were far from that of postgraduates.

In one hand, higher education was participated in by 29,665 graduates in comparison with only 2,725 postgraduates. In addition, the figure for graduate students doing part-time jobs was roughly six times higher than that of postgraduates which were 17,735 and 2,535 students respectively.

On the other hand, there were 345 postgraduate students working as volunteers after their study. This number was about nine times less than that of further study in the same education level, and 10 times when compared with this number of graduate students. Moreover, the unemployed figure for postgraduates was 1,625 people compared with 16,235 graduates. Those figures were approximately a half of the number of higher education in its chart.

173 words

MODEL ANSWER 2:

The two bar charts illustrate the figures of UK graduate and postgraduate students in terms of employment excluding full-time work after graduation in 2008.

Overall, the highest number of graduate students pursued to study further, whereas further study and part-time work were the two most common choices of postgraduates in the same year.

Looking at the first graph, graduate students studying further took the lead, holding exact 29,665 students of the total surveyed. Following this, 17,735 students choosing part-time work, which was marginally higher than that of students who are unemployed (16,235). However, the least common choice was voluntary work with just 3500 students.

Turning to the second graph, the greatest figure of postgraduate students was represented by further study, followed by part-time work with the figures of 2725 and 2535 respectively. The number of unemployed students was just over half of that of further study, at 1625 compared to 2725. Lastly, there were only 345 students joining voluntary work, which made it the least popular choice among four groups.

170 words

SAMPLE 37

The table below shows the number of cars per hour crossing the four major bridges in New Stratford at 8 a.m., 12 noon, 4 p.m., 8 p.m., and midnight.

Summarise the information by selecting and reporting the main features, and make comparisons where relevant.

Write at least 150 words.

Bridges	8 a.m.	12 Noon	4 p.m.	8 p.m.	Midnight
Harbour Bridge	12,500	10,300	11,750	6,400	2,550
River Bridge	8,300	6,490	8,500	4,450	1,250
City Bridge	6,225	6,800	6,150	1,280	555
Smith Bridge	2,350	2,125	3,330	1,225	430

The table reveals the number of cars joining the traffic on four main bridges in New Stratford in five different time frames.

It is evident that 8 a.m., 12 noon and 4 p.m. are the three points of time attracting more cars than two remaining ones.

The traffic on the Harbour Bridge is the heaviest at 8 a.m. with 12,500 cars, while 4 p.m. is the second busiest time with 11,750 cars. Likewise, traffic on the River Bridge is the most crowded at 8 a.m. and 4 p.m. with 8,300 and 8,500 cars respectively. However, in the evening, traffic density is reduced considerably for both two bridges. In particular, the total traffic volume at 8 p.m. and midnight of Habour and River Bridge is about 9,000 and 6000 cars respectively.

As for two remaining bridges, at 6,800 cars, the City Bridge is used the most at noon, whereas 4 p.m. is the busiest time for the Smith Bridge with 3,330 cars. At night, the number of cars crossing/passing these two bridges reduced significantly, with lower-than-600 cars for each. What is also noteworthy is that/It is also noteworthy that in terms of usage, the Harbour, River, City and Smith bridge is the first, second, third and last respectively.

207 words

SAMPLE 38

The graph below shows the quantities of goods transported in the UK between 1974 and 2002 by four different modes of transport.

Summarise the information by selecting and reporting the main features, and make comparisons where relevant.

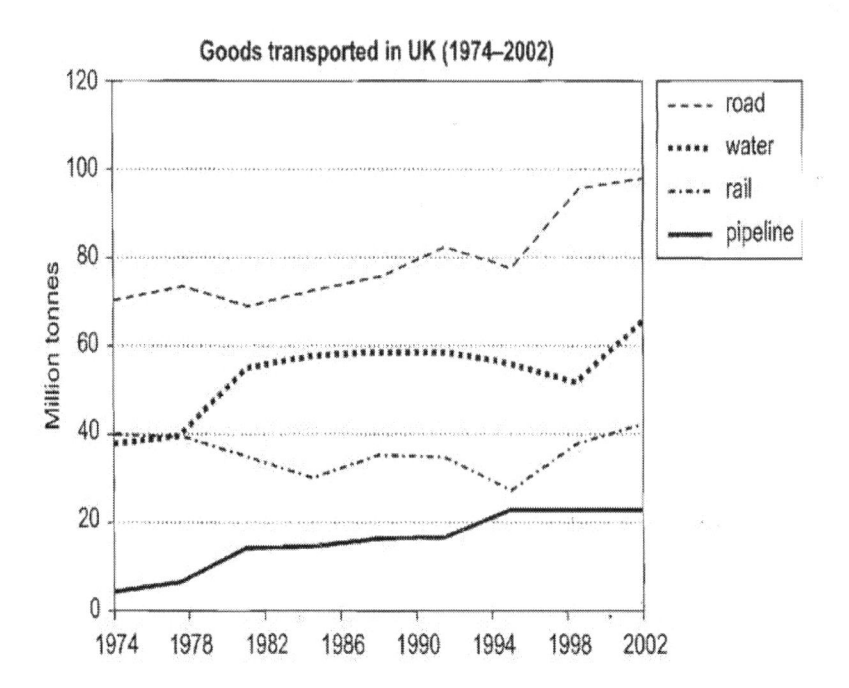

MODEL ANSWER 1:

The line graph provides information about the quantities of products transported in the UK from 1974 to 2002 by four different types of transport.

Overall, there was a gradual rise in the quantities of goods transported for all transport despite some fluctuations. It is also clear to see that transporting by road accounted for the highest proportion of the quantities of product over the period of 28 years.

In the year 1974, the quantity of goods transported by road was about 71 million tonnes. Throughout the remainder of the period, there was a fluctuation in products transported and then it rose to approximately 98 million tonnes in 2002. The quantities of goods transported by both water and rail had the same starting point at 38 million tonnes in the year 1974. Furthermore, despite having different patterns from 1978 to 1983, both showed the same trend afterward but the figures for water were always higher than those for rail. By 2002, the quantities of water and rail increased to 62 and 41 million tonnes, respectively.

There was a gradual rise in good transported by pipeline which was always the lowest figure at under 20 million tonnes from 1974 to 2002. Specifically, in 1974 the quantity was about 4 million tones and it increased to 21 million tonnes in 2002 after two stable periods from 1983 to 1990 and from 1994 to 2002.

220 words

MODEL ANSWER 2:

The line graph compares the number of consumer wares transported by four major means of transport in the UK from 1974 to 2002.

Overall, road played a key role in the transportation of commodities, whereas pipeline experienced an opposite side in the UK during the given period. As can be seen that, the number of goods transported by road, water and pipeline saw a significant rise while the figure for rail remained stable.

From 1974 to 1978, the quantities of goods delivered on road fluctuated, although it always remained above 70 million, which was the highest figure. At the same time, pipeline experienced a slight upward trend in the number of goods transportations, rising between 5 and approximately 15 million tonnes. Over the next two decades, the figure of using roads for transporting reached a peak rocketed to the high of almost 100 million. Likewise, the number of wares transported by pipeline increased significantly, leaping to over 20 million at the end of the period.

From under 40 million tonnes, the quantities of commodities delivered on water was steadily lower than the figure for rail, at 40 million in 1974. After 4 years, of goods transported by ships climbed to 40 million then rocketed to the high of above 60 million. In contrast, there was a fluctuating trend of using rail to transport goods during the given period but came back at 40 million in 2002.

219 words

SAMPLE 39

The line graph shows the sales of children's books, adult's fictions and educational books between 2002 and 2006 in one country.

Summarise the information by selecting and reporting the main features, and make comparisons where relevant.

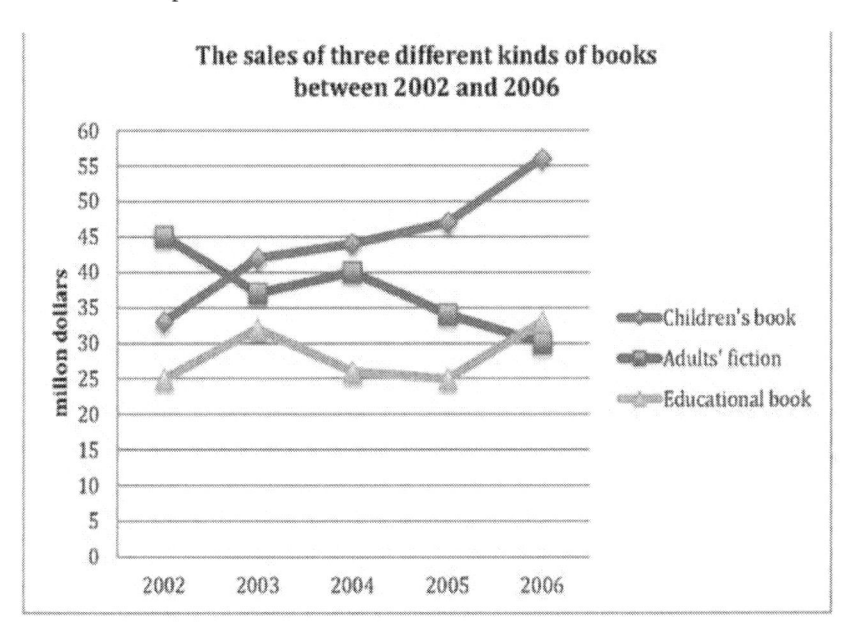

The graph gives information about the amount of money people get from selling three different kinds of books in a country from 2002 to 2006.

Overall, the sales of children's books and educational books were similar in terms of a general increase over the period of 5 years, while the figure for adult's books experienced a moderate decline. In addition, among three different kinds of books, children's books were by far the most popular.

In the 2003 – 2004 period, the revenue from both books for kids and books for education went up significantly, from about 33 to 42 million dollars and exactly 25 to 32 million dollars respectively. In contrast, there was a considerable decrease in the number of adults' fiction, which dropped to around 37 million dollars.

The remainder of the period witnessed a gradual growth of 10 million dollars in the sales of children's books. Likewise, there was a sharp rise from 25 to approximately 33 million dollars in the sales of educational books in the year 2006 after a slight decrease of 7 million dollars between 2003 and 2005. On the contrary, after rising from nearly 37 to 40 million dollars in the year 2004, the figure for adults' fictions went down noticeably, falling to 30 million dollars in 2006.

213 words

SAMPLE 40

The line graph below gives information about the number of visitors to three London museums between June and September 2013.

Summarise the information by selecting and reporting the main features, and make comparisons where relevant.

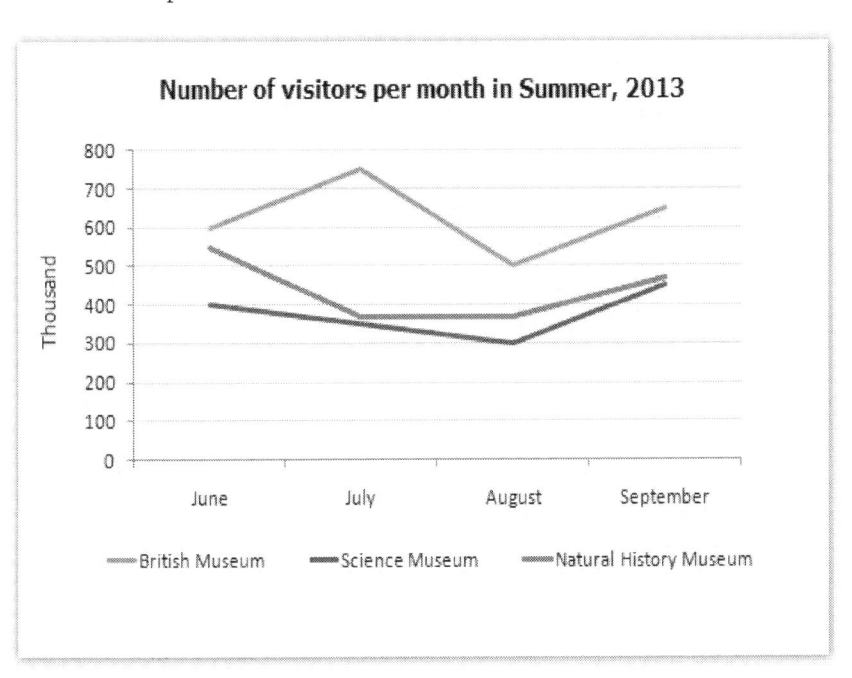

MODEL ANSWER 1:

The chart compares the number of people coming to visit three different types of museums in London from June to September 2013.

Overall, British Museum was the most popular museum in London, which serviced the largest number of visitors in summer 2013. In contrast, the number of people visiting Science Museum ranked the lowest figure but it had an increasing trend in the end of summer.

Over the period from June to July, there was a dramatic growth in the number of British museum's visitors reaching a peak at approximately 750 thousand. However, the trend of visiting this museum saw a rapid fell, reaching the lowest data at exactly 500 thousand people. Finally, from

August, the number of visitor coming to British museum rose significantly, at about 650 thousand in the end of summer.

Natural History museum experienced a sharp decrease in the number of visitors from June to July then this figure grew slightly, at about 500 thousand in September. The number of Science museum's visitor dropped rapidly between Jun and August, but it had an upward trend, at 450 thousand visitors.

183 words

MODEL ANSWER 2:

The graph shows data about how many people visited the three London museums from June to September 2013.

Overall, the number of visitors to the three different Museums fluctuated widely during a period of four months. However, most visitors went to the British Museum while the other Museums received fewer visitors.

It is clear from the graph that the number of visitors to British Museum rose sharply from 600 thousand to around 750 thousand within a month. After that, it fell rapidly to just under 500 thousand before growing again to about 650 thousand.

When it comes to the Natural History Museum, the number of people visited this place declined significantly from just under 500 thousand to around 370 thousand in the first month the survey conducted then climbed slightly to around 470 thousand within the next two months. It can be seen from the line graph that there was a similar trend for Science Museum. Starting at 400 thousand people, it decreased steadily to just over 300 thousand over a two-month period before climbing suddenly to 450 thousand in the next month.

183 words

SAMPLE 41

The graphs below show a comparison of the expenses in the UK and the US.

Expenses in the UK   Expenses in the US

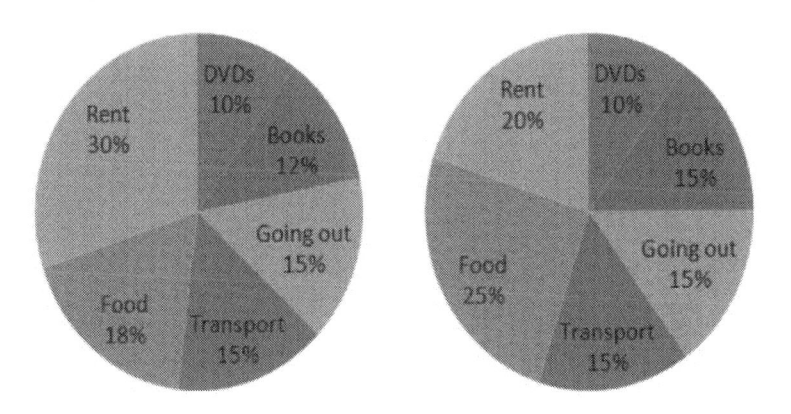

The pie charts compare the percentages of expenditure in terms of six different categories: DVDs, Books, Going out, Transport, Food and Rent in two countries UK and US.

It is clear that people spend the most money on Rent and Food in both countries. By contrast, the expenses for DVDs is the least.

The percentage of spending on DVDs is 10%, while the figure for Books is slightly higher, at 12%. At the same time, spending on going out and transport in the UK each makes up 15% of the total expense. Meanwhile, expenditure on Food accounts for 18% of the total money spent by British people. By contrast, the rate of spending on Rent stands at 30%, which was the highest figure.

In the US, the proportion of expense on DVDs is as high as the figure for the UK, at 10%. People in America spend an analogous percentage of its budget on three categories: Books, Going out, Transport, standing at 15%. At the same time, money spent on Food makes up a quarter of the total expenditure in this country, which is the highest compared to other five categories. Meanwhile, 20% is spent on Rent, which is 2 times higher than the percentage of DVDs.

207 words

SAMPLE 42

The graph below shows radio and television audiences of United Kingdom throughout the day in the year 1992.

Write a report for a university lecturer describing the information shown below.

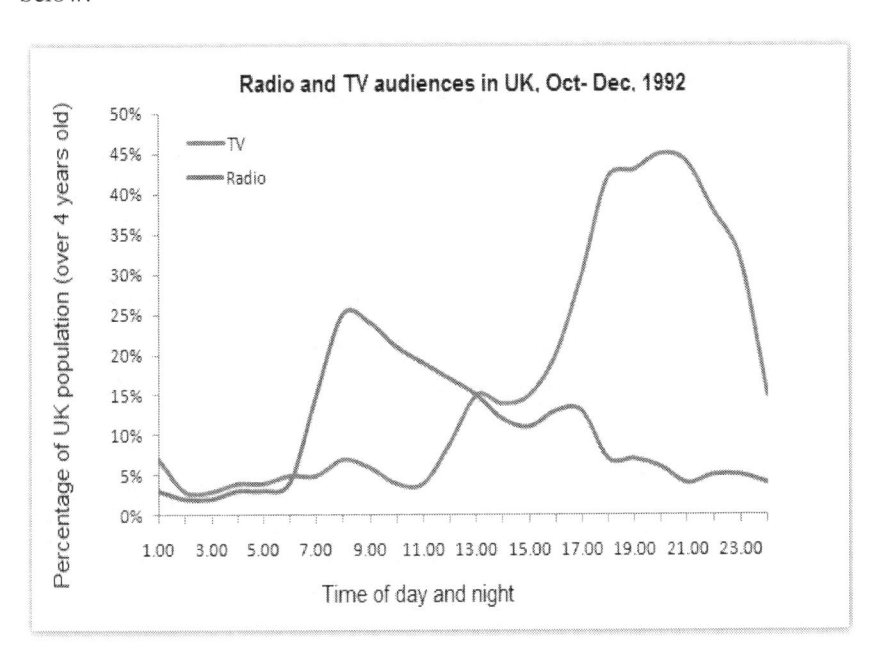

The line graph compares changes in the daily proportion of people who listen to the radio or watch television in 1992 in England.

Overall, the rate of British users in both media fluctuated wildly over 22 hours in 1992. Besides the completely different trends, the percentage of television audiences in most years was higher than that of radio.

From 1.00 to 2.00, TV viewers rate fell quickly although it was still higher than radio audiences rate at that same time (7% fell closely to 3%) in the UK. Nevertheless, in the 2.00-8.00 period, the quantity of those who watch televisions improve modestly to approximate 6%. From 8.00 to 13.00, the figure for television had a slight trough and then recovered to above 15%. Throughout the remainder of the period, there was a slide-back change in the television watchers ratio, which reached the maximum rate at 45% but then fell sharply back to 15% at the end of the day.

Over the same period, the rate of radio audiences vacillated less outrageously than that of television watcher rate. It remained almost constant over the first five-hour period before peaking at above 25%, its highest point, in the next short two hours. By contrast, there was a gradual drop (from over 25% to under 5%) during the rest of the day in the number of people who listen to the radio in the UK in 1992.

233 words

SAMPLE 43

The charts below show UK and USA energy consumption in 2000 and 2006.

Summarise the information by selecting and reporting the main features, and make comparisons where relevant.

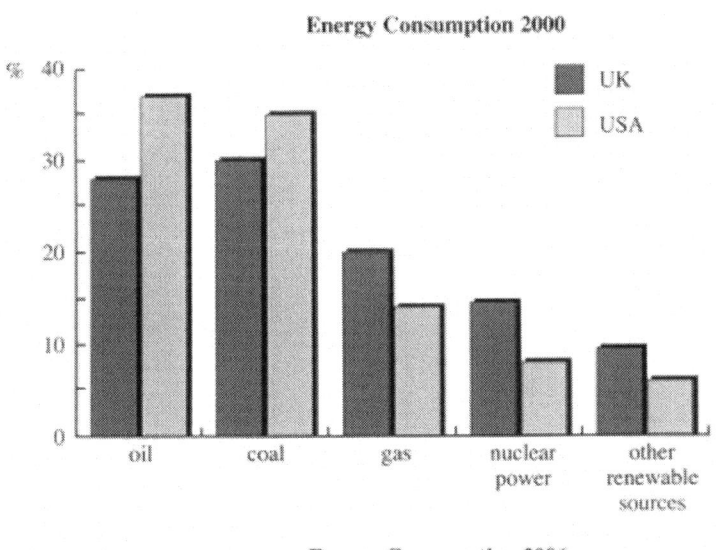

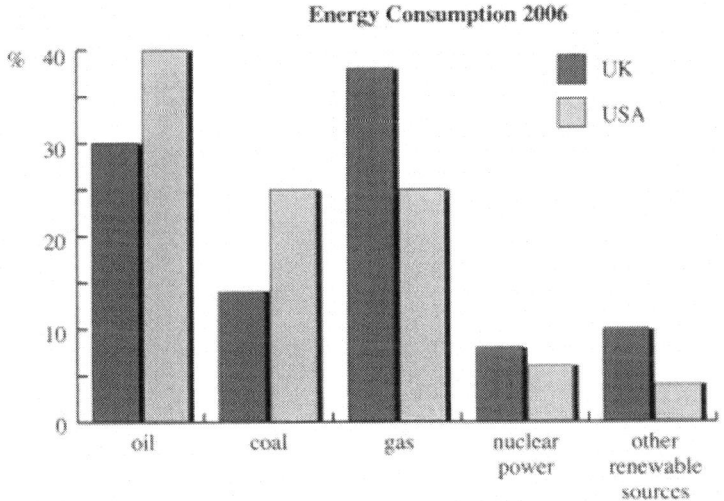

The charts compare the energy expenditure in the UK and USA by the years 2000 and 2006

Overall, oil was the most used energy source in both countries, and the energy consumption in the UK was generally greater than in the USA over the period

In 2000, the energy consumption in both countries derived primarily from oil and coal. These figures, however, were slightly higher in American, at around 35% in the USA and 30% in the UK. By contrast, the British consumed steadily more energy than American in the remainder of energy sources including gas, nuclear power, and other sources.

Six years later, oil still remained relatively to be the most popular fuel generation in the USA with precisely 40% in consumption, while the amount of gas used increased considerably in both countries and was highest in the UK, at nearly 40% in 2006. Coal consumption experienced a significant decrease in the UK and UAS, accounting for extremely 15% and 255 respectively, while the expenditure of nuclear power and other sources declined slightly throughout the period.

177 words

SAMPLE 44

The chart below gives information on the percentage of British people giving money to charity by age range for the years 1990 and 2010.

Summarise the information by selecting and reporting the main features and make comparisons where relevant.

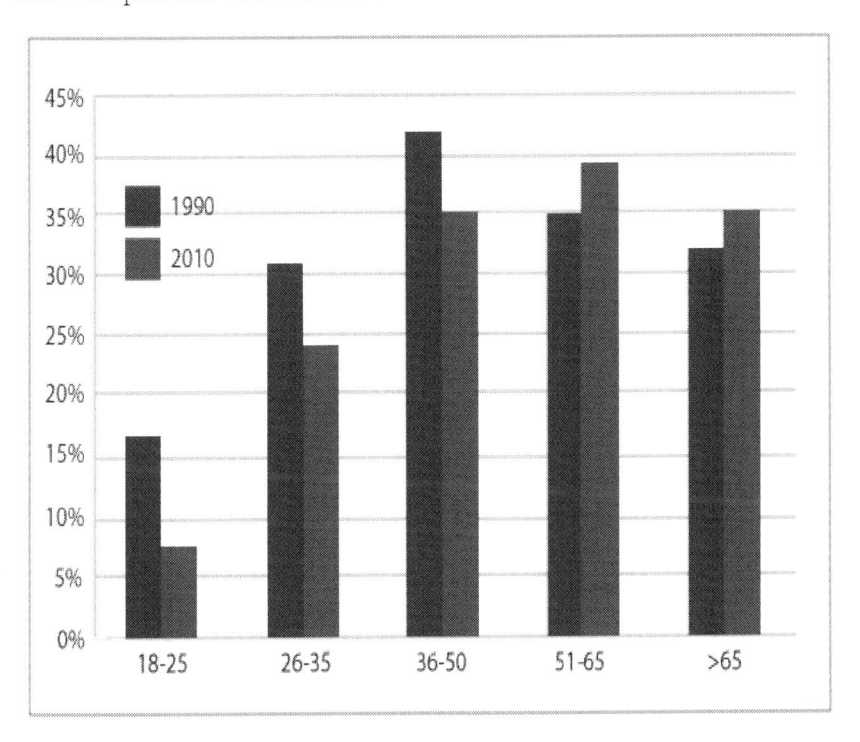

The bar chart illustrates data on the proportion of Britons donating money to charity by five different age groups in 1990 and 2010.

Overall, the percentage of British citizens giving money to charity in 3 age groups 18-25, 26-35 and 36-50 in 1990 was higher than that in 2010 while the figures for 2 other groups in 1990 were lower than the rates in 2010. The highest point of the year 1990 was at the age of 36-50 and the one of the year 2010 was the 51-65 age group.

In 1990, the proportion of Britons at the age of 18-25 spending money on charity was the lowest, at around 17%. By contrast, the figure for the group

36-50 was the highest, at about 42%. Approximately 31%, 35% and 32% British people donated money to charity in 3 age group 26-35, 51-65 and over 65, respectively.

In 2010, the proportion of British citizens spending money on charity at the age of 51-65 was the highest, at around 39% while the figures for 2 groups 36-50 and over 65 were the same. The rate for the 18-25 age group was the lowest.

191 words

SAMPLE 45

The charts below show the number of Japanese tourists travelling abroad between 1985 and 1995 and Australia's share of the Japanese tourist market.

Summarise the information by selecting and reporting the main features, and make comparisons where relevant.

Source: https://www.testbig.com/ielts-writing-task-i-ielts-academic-essays/charts-below-show-number-japanese-tourists-travelling-2

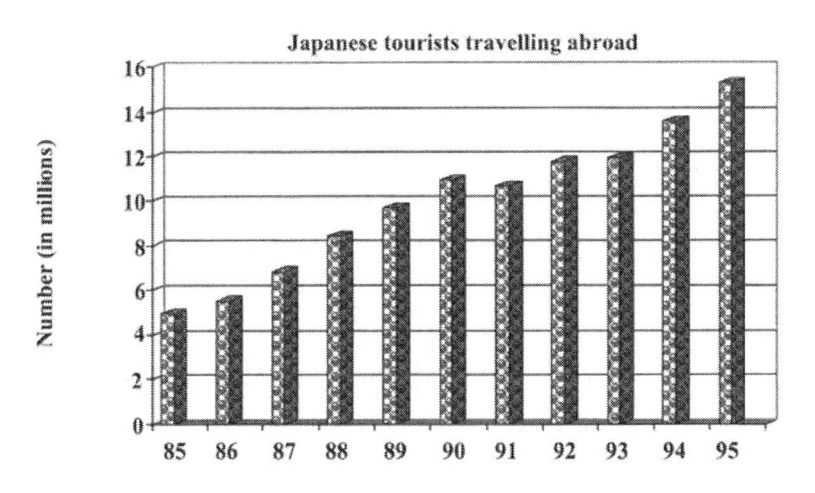

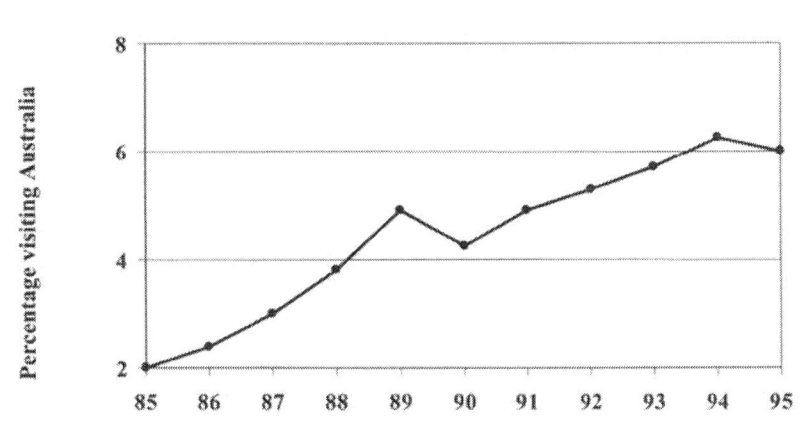

The bar chart compares the quantity of Japanese tourists who travelled abroad and the line graph gives information about Australia's share of the Japanese tourist market over the ten-year period from 1985 to 1995.

It is clear that the number of Japanese tourists travelling abroad increased gradually over the period shown. Meanwhile, there was an upward trend in the percentage of Japanese tourists visiting Australia.

In 1985, there were about 5 million individuals travelling overseas in Japan. From 1985 to 1990, there was a gradual rise in the number of Japanese tourists to 11 million. Then this figure experienced a slow drop to just under 11 million in 1991. After that, the number of tourists rose steadily and reached a peak at more than 15 million in 1995.

The percentage of Japanese visitors coming to Australia was 2% in 1985. This figure kept rising for the next four years and reached 5% in 1989. After that, there was a slight decline in the proportion of tourists to more than 4% in 1990. From 1990 to 1994, Australia's share of the Japanese tourist market increased dramatically and reached the highest point of over 6% in 1994. Then this figure witnessed a slight drop to 6% in 1995.

206 words

SAMPLE 46

The charts below give information on the ages of the population of Yemen and Italy in 2000 and projections for 2050.

Summarise the information by selecting and reporting the main features, and make comparisons where relevant.

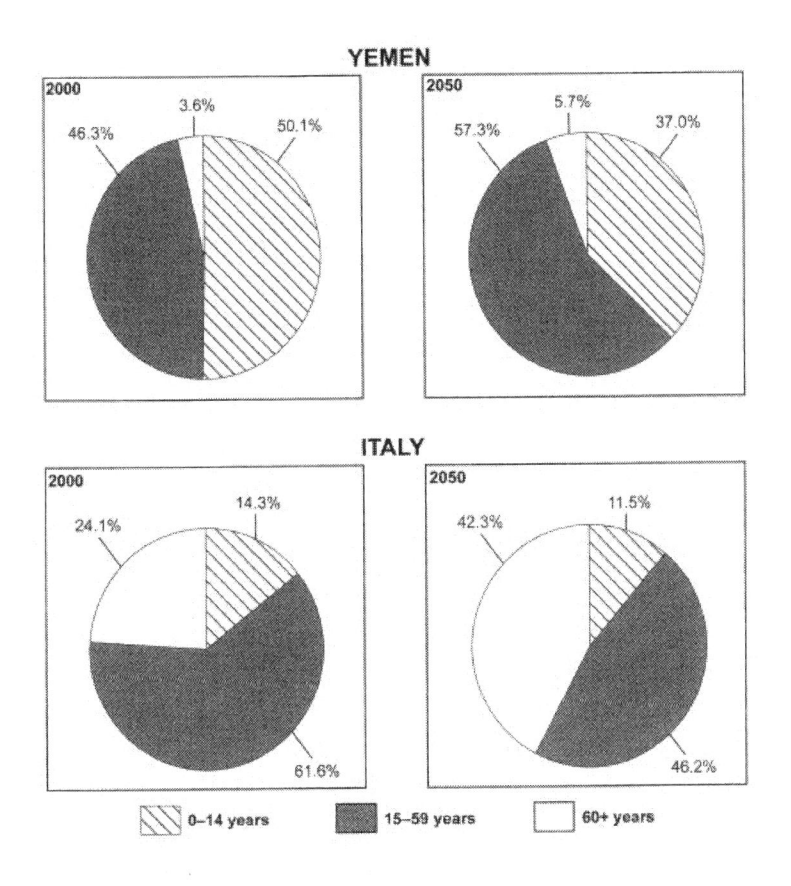

<u>**MODEL ANSWER 1:**</u>

The charts given demonstrate the data on three age groups of ages in Yemen and Italy over 50 years from 2000 to 2050.

Overall, Italy had a more aging population than that of Yemen throughout the period shown. It is also noticeable that people in both countries become older over 50 years.

In 2000, while juveniles under 14 accounted for half of Yemen's population, only one-third of that amount was the proportion of children under 14 years old in Italy. Meanwhile, the middle age group of ages ranging from 15 to 59 years old in Yemen took up over 46% of the population, while that figure in Italy was around 15% more. Besides, the elderly aged 60 and over in Yemen had a tiny percentage at 3.6%; however, in Italy the elderly comprised up to about a quarter of its population.

By 2050, the population of both countries will have experienced the aging process. Specifically, in Yemen, the figure for juveniles will decrease by 13%, and that for the middle group will rise to almost 60% simultaneously. Nonetheless, the old group aged over 60 will show a modest increase of only 2%. On the other hand, in Italy, the young group witnessed just a slight decline in percentage, whereas the middle group will fall to 46% and the figure for old people will rise by around 20%. As can be seen, Yemen is predicted to undergo a slower aging process than that of Italy.

220 words

MODEL ANSWER 2:

The pie charts provide information on the aged groups of citizens of Yemen and Italy in 2000 and predictions for 2050.

Overall, the most significant age group is from 15-59 years, which accounts for over half the national ages, while other groups generated the least statistics in Yemen and Italy.

In 2000, with the age group from 15-59 years, Yemen people took 46.3% less than those of Italian with 61.6%. When it comes to 0-14 years group, the figures for Yemen and Italy were 50.1% and 14.3% respectively. Meanwhile, the 60-year group represented 3.6% of Yemen population and 24.1% of Italy citizens.

With regards to the projections for 2050, the labor aged 15-59 years in Yemen will significantly increase to 57.3 % while in this group, the percentage of the ages in Italy is anticipated to fall dramatically to 46.2%. The figure for people in the 0-14 group is forecast to drop to 57% in Yemen and 11.5% in Italy. However, the eldest aged group in Yemen and Italy is expected to rise to 5.7% and 42.3% respectively.

178 words

SAMPLE 47

WRITING TASK 1

You should spend about 20 minutes on this task.

> *The pie charts below give information about the household expenditure of two*
> *average U.S. families in different years.*
> *Summarise the information by selecting and reporting the main features, and make*
> *comparisons where relevant.*

Write at least 150 words.

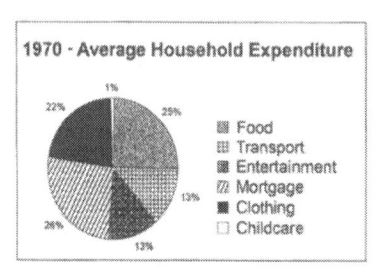 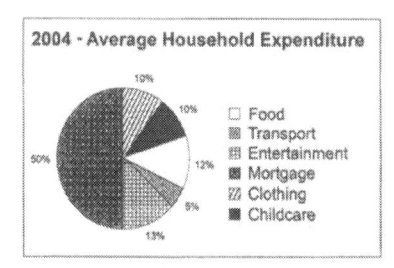

The pie charts compare the percentages of average spending of two different U.S. families in 1970 and 2004.

Overall, U.S. families tended to spend more on mortgage in both years. While mortgage saw a drastic increase from 1970 to 2004, the relative amount of total household spending for other categories either remained unchanged or dropped.

In 1970, mortgage made up 26% of average household expenditure. The figure for this category doubled in 2004, taking up half of household spending. Food held the second place in 1970, at 25%. However, the relative amount of food significantly dropped to 12% in 2004.

Similar to food, clothing, and transport experienced a decrease in the relative amount of average household expenditure, from 22% and 13% to 10% and 5% respectively. The percentage of spending for entertainment remained the same at 13%. By contrast, the proportion of childcare spending rose 10 times, from 1% to 10%.

152 words

SAMPLE 48

The pie charts below give information about the composition of household rubbish in the United Kingdom in two different years.

Summarise the information by selecting and reporting the main features, and make comparisons where relevant.

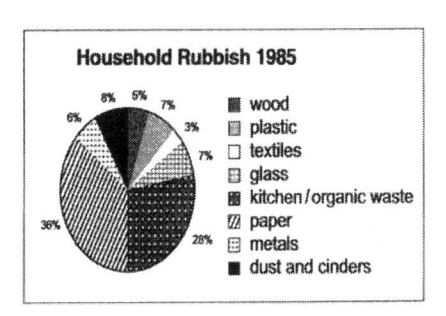 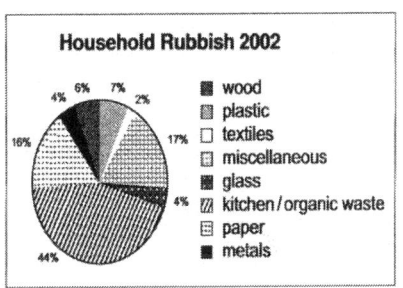

The pie charts show the data on different components of household rubbish in the United Kingdom in 1985 and 2002.

Overall, the percentage of most components of household rubbish remained stable from 1985 to 2002 apart from kitchen/organic waste and paper. Moreover, dust and cinders were disappeared and miscellaneous were added in 2002.

The percentage of kitchen/organic waste jumped from 28% in 1985 to 44% in 2002, which represented the biggest increase in that period of time. By contrast, paper waste was significantly reduced from 36% to 16% in 1985 and in 2002, respectively.

The proportion of plastic waste remained the same in both years, at 7%. The UK's household rubbish in 1985 saw a similar figure for wood with 5% and textile with 3%. The miscellaneous which did not appear in 1985 represented 17%, while dust and cinders which were at 8% in household rubbish in 1985, disappeared in 2002.

151 words

SAMPLE 49

The graph and table below give information about water use worldwide and water consumption in two different countries.

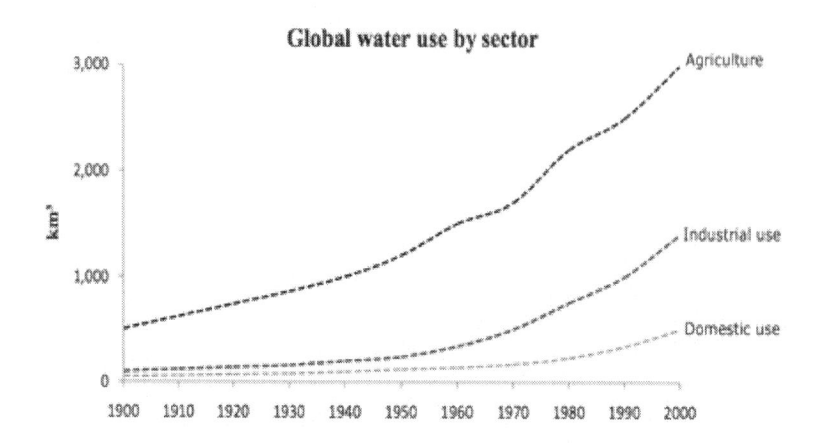

Global water use by sector

Water consumption in Brazil and Congo in 2000

Country	Population	Irrigated land	Water consumption per person
Brazil	176 million	26,500 km²	359 m³
Democratic Republic of Congo	5.2 million	100 km²	8 m³

MODEL ANSWER 1:

The charts show the comparison between the amount of water consumed for Agriculture, Industry, and homes, all over the World from 1900 to 2000, and water used in Brazil and Congo in 2000.

Overall, the common trend for global water consumption was upward. Moreover, a much larger amount of water was used for Agriculture in comparison with Industry and Domestic use, and Brazilians consumed more water than people living in Congo.

In 1900, water was used mainly for agriculture with about 500 km3 when

Industrial use and homes made up for over 10 km3. By 2000, the amount of water for agricultural consumption soared significantly by 3,000 km3 which were approximately 2,000 km3 more than that in Industrial use. The Domestic use experienced the same trend through the period shown with a gradual rise by around 400 km3 in 2000.

It is easily seen that there was a huge gap between the population of Brazil and Democratic Republic of Congo which was 176 million compared with 5.2 million respectively. The agricultural land in Brazil was approximately twenty-seven times more than that in Congo. Therefore/Correspondingly, the figure for water consumption per person in Congo was 45 times less than Brazilian residents used which were 8 m3 and 359 m3 respectively.

209 words

MODEL ANSWER 2:

A glance at the charts provided reveals the amount of global water used for agriculture, industry, and home from 1900 to 2000 and water use in two countries namely Brazil and Democratic of Congo in 2000.

It is apparent that agricultural purpose was responsible for the largest proportion of water globally used which rose dramatically during the 20th century. It can be also seen from the table that Brazilian utilized more water significantly than Congolese.

In 1900, there were approximately 500 km3 of water used in agriculture which was more five times more than that in domestic and industry. Although the amount of water used in three areas all witnessed a remarkable growth in the surveyed period, water consumption in agriculture was still the highest with 3,000 km3 in 2000. By contrast, domestic sector, which consumed nearly 500 km3 of water, stood at the bottom of global water use while 1,000 km3 was the amount of water for the industry in 2000.

In the same year, the population of Brazil and Congo were 176 million and 5.2 million respectively. As a result, water consumption per person in Brazil at 359 m3 was much higher than in Congo at only 8 m3. It can be easy to understand it because the former had more 265 times irrigated land than the latter.

220 words

SAMPLE 50

The pie charts below show units of electricity production by fuel source Australia and France in 1980 and 2000.

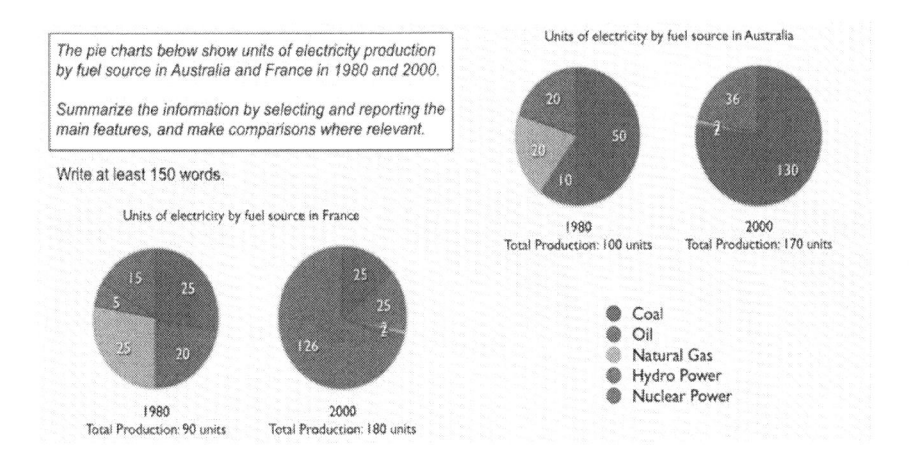

The pie charts below show units of electricity production by fuel source in Australia and France in 1980 and 2000.

Summarize the information by selecting and reporting the main features, and make comparisons where relevant.

Write at least 150 words.

Units of electricity by fuel source in France

1980 — Total Production: 90 units
2000 — Total Production: 180 units

Units of electricity by fuel source in Australia

1980 — Total Production: 100 units
2000 — Total Production: 170 units

- Coal
- Oil
- Natural Gas
- Hydro Power
- Nuclear Power

MODEL ANSWER 1:

The pie charts compare the amount of electricity produced by different sources of fuels in Australia and France in 2 separate years 1980 and 2000.

Overall, it is clear that there was a rise in the total amount of electricity production in both 2 countries in 2000. The majority electricity was produced by coal and hydropower in Australia, and by nuclear power in France in 2000.

As can be seen, in 1980 in Australia, coal accounted for the highest figure, at 50 units, whereas hydro and nuclear power had the similar number, at 20 units. However, these figures are much higher than the amount of electricity produced by oil, at only 10 units. The year 2000 witnessed an increase in the amount electricity produced by coal at 130 units, compared to 36 units of hydropower.

In France, the main sources produced electricity in 1980 were coal and natural gas, at 25 units, whereas oil's figure was slightly lower by 5 units. In 2000, there was a dramatic increase in the amount of electricity by nuclear to 126 units. Meanwhile, oil and coal had the same figures, at 25 units. The figures for hydropower and natural gas fall significantly, at 2 units for both categories.

204 words

<u>**MODEL ANSWER 2:**</u>

The pie charts demonstrate the electricity amount produced from five different sources of fuel in Australia and France in 1980 and 2000.

Overall, both countries experienced a dramatic increase in total electricity production from 1980 to 2000. Also, coal and nuclear power were the main fuel sources to produce electricity in Australia and France respectively in 2000.

In 1980, only 50 units of coal were used for electricity producing in Australia, but the number remarkably jumped to 130 units in 2000. This country also witnessed a gradual rise in the electricity units using hydropower. In contrast, producing electricity from oil and natural gas dramatically dropped from 10 and 20 units respectively in 1980 to only 2 units each in 2000.

In France, while electric power generated from coal and oil sources was constant at around 25 units during the 20-year period, the amount derived from nuclear power predominated with 126 units in 2000. However, there was a significant decrease in electricity production from natural gas from 25 to only 2 units in 2000.

173 words

CONCLUSION

Thank you again for downloading this book on *"IELTS Academic Writing Task 1 Samples: 50 High Quality Samples for Your Reference to Gain a High Band Score 8.0+ in 1 Week (Book 9)."* and reading all the way to the end. I'm extremely grateful.

If you know of anyone else who may benefit from the useful task 1 writing sample essays for their reference, please help me inform them of this book. I would greatly appreciate it.

Finally, if you enjoyed this book and feel that it has added value to your work and study in any way, please take a couple of minutes to share your thoughts and post a REVIEW on Amazon. Your feedback will help me to continue to write other books of IELTS topic that helps you get the best results. Furthermore, if you write a simple REVIEW with positive words for this book on Amazon, you can help hundreds or perhaps thousands of other readers who may want to improve their English writing skills sounding like a native speaker. Like you, they worked hard for every penny they spend on books. With the information and recommendation you provide, they would be more likely to take action right away. We really look forward to reading your review.

Thanks again for your support and good luck!

If you enjoy my book, please write a POSITIVE REVIEW on Amazon.

-- Rachel Mitchell --

CHECK OUT OTHER BOOKS

Go here to check out other related books that might interest you:

Shortcut To English Collocations: Master 2000+ English Collocations In Used Explained Under 20 Minutes A Day (5 books in 1 Box set)

https://www.amazon.com/dp/B06W2P6S22

IELTS Writing Task 1 + 2: The Ultimate Guide with Practice to Get a Target Band Score of 8.0+ In 10 Minutes a Day

https://www.amazon.com/dp/B075DFYPG6

IELTS Speaking Strategies: The Ultimate Guide With Tips, Tricks, And Practice On How To Get A Target Band Score Of 8.0+ In 10 Minutes A Day.

https://www.amazon.com/dp/B075JCW65G

Shortcut To Ielts Writing: The Ultimate Guide To Immediately Increase Your Ielts Writing Scores.

https://www.amazon.com/dp/B01JV7EQGG

Common English Mistakes Explained With Examples: Over 600
Mistakes Almost Students Make and How to Avoid Them in Less
Than 5 Minutes A Day

https://www.amazon.com/dp/B072PXVHNZ

**Paraphrasing Strategies: 10 Simple Techniques For Effective
Paraphrasing In 5 Minutes Or Less**

https://www.amazon.com/dp/B071DFG27Q

Legal Vocabulary In Use: Master 600+ Essential Legal Terms And Phrases Explained In 10 Minutes A Day

http://www.amazon.com/dp/B01L0FKXPU

Legal Terminology And Phrases: Essential Legal Terms Explained
You Need To Know About Crimes, Penalty And Criminal Procedure

http://www.amazon.com/dp/B01L5EB54Y

Productivity Secrets For Students: The Ultimate Guide To Improve Your Mental Concentration, Kill Procrastination, Boost Memory And Maximize Productivity In Study

http://www.amazon.com/dp/B01JS52UT6

Daughter of Strife: 7 Techniques On How To Win Back Your
Stubborn Teenage Daughter

https://www.amazon.com/dp/B01HS5E3V6

Parenting Teens With Love And Logic: A Survival Guide To Overcoming The Barriers Of Adolescence About Dating, Sex And Substance Abuse

https://www.amazon.com/dp/B01JQUTNPM

http://www.amazon.com/dp/B01K0ARNA4

Printed in Great Britain
by Amazon

32552880R00076